Dear Dennis & Betty,

Enjoy Quanzhou,

Yours

Dr. Bill
& Family

Executive Editor: Shi Gaoxiang   施高翔
Cover & Illustrations: Dr. William N. Brown   Wen Xin   潘维廉   文心

Mystic Quanzhou

魅力泉州

Dr. Bill Brown

魅力老潘

厦门大学出版社
Xiamen University Press

Ancient Garden City

(These 4 pages of photos compliments of master photographer Chen Sizhe)

Garden Community

Twin Pagodas

Prized Miniature Landscapes

East Lake Park

West Lake (the "Western Ocean")

Photographer Chen Sizhe

Chen Sizhe
Hui'an Maiden

Chen Sizhe
Traditional Minnan (S. Fujian) Village

Chen Sizhe
300-year-old Bridge

Chen Sizhe
Confucian Literary Temple

Chen Sizhe
Quanzhou's "Great Wall"

Chen Sizhe
Marco I

Chen Sizhe
Historic Zhongshan Rd. Restoration Project

Bamboo Rafting in Dehua

Art in the Park

Fowl Play

Nightscape

One of 407 Protected Ancient Trees

Ancient Canal

UNESCO's "Excellent Relic Protection in Asia-Pacific Area, 2001"

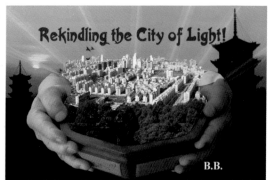

Rekindling the City of Light!

B.B.

Growing but Greening

The New Maritime Silk Road

"City in the Garden, Garden in the City"

Who's pulling whose strings?

City set amidst mountains, rivers and the sea

Ancient Zaytun's
Rich and Diverse Heritage

Origin of Anxi Tea and Tea Ceremony

Ancient Biological Engineering!

Home of S. Chinese Music

Source of Legendary Porcelain

Start of the Maritime Silk Road

Birthplace of S. Shaolin Kung Fu   **Home of Chinese Puppetry**

UNESCO
"World Museum of Religion"

Judaism　**Nestorian**

Taoism

Hinduism

Confucianism

Manichaeanism　**Christianity**

Tibetan Buddhism

Ashab Mosque

Islam

Garden Architecture

Protected Trees Amidst
"New Classic" Architecture

Zaytun's Walls Rise Again!
Downtown Project

Before

Ancient Minnan Architecture, Hi-Tech Solar Heating

and...

After!

Shopping Area Near Ashab Mosque

New Residential District

New Apartment Building

Quanzhou Cuisine

Shark lips!

Fish 'n crispy rice

Mystic Quanzhou
City of Light[1]

Comments, suggestions, questions, corrections, or requests for copies of Mystic Quanzhou at bulk corporate and educational discounts? **E-mail:**
bbrown@public.xm.fj.cn

Snail mail:
Dr. Bill Brown,
Box 1288, Xiamen University
Xiamen, Fujian, PRC 361005

Complaints? Write my wife, Susan Marie! And check her website for Updates!

http://www.amoymagic.com

---

[1] "The City of Lights" is the title of Selbourne's translation of the memoirs of Jacob D'Ancona, a Jewish merchant who supposedly visited China 4 years before Marco Polo. True or not, it's a fascinating story, and I like the name "City of Light" for several reasons: Quanzhou, start of the Maritime Silk Road, was a commercial and cultural crossroads, a great melting pot, with people of all nations and faiths living together peacefully—a true light in that era, and one that I hope to see rekindled.

Preface

When former Fujian Governor Xi Jinping saw *Amoy Magic*, he suggested I also write about my "3rd Home" as well (Xiamen being my 2nd, and I'm not sure where my 1st is). That was 3 years ago and only this summer did I have time to put this together. I wrote *Mystic Quanzhou* in only six weeks, between semesters, and it probably shows it. But I hope that in spite of the book's shortcomings, it will help you better appreciate, and enjoy, one of China's most fascinating cities—especially for foreigners. (And as always… e-mail me with your corrections, suggestions, and additions).

Quanzhou, the ancient start of the Maritime Silk Road, has changed dramatically since my first visit in January, 1989. In fact, over the past two decades Quanzhou was #3 in economic growth amongst China's biggest 212 cities. But happily, perhaps more than any other Chinese city, Quanzhou balanced phenomenal growth with preservation and enhancement of an unparalleled historical, cultural and natural heritage.

Quanzhou did not just save (store away!) her heritage but actually incorporated it into the new city. For example, all new architecture, whether apartment buildings, banks or shopping malls, must follow codes that insure the historical and cultural aesthetics of each district. The result is a uniquely modern, comfortable city that embraces the future while preserving a colorful past—a feat that has won the city kudos from UNESCO's Relic Protection Campaign, as well as honors for environmental protection. Quite a city!

While Quanzhou changes constantly, it manages to retain and even strengthen the identity that so enthralled Marco Polo and others. And the more I understand Quanzhou, the more I suspect that both Columbus and Marco Polo totally overlooked the true wealth of this beautiful place and people…

Zaytun Treasures

Dr. Bill Brown
Xiamen, China
August 2003

Acknowledgements

Thank you, Susan, Shannon and Matthew (my wife and two sons) for your patience as I raced to piece this book together. I hope I did not leave my family in pieces while doing it!

Many thanks to the exuberant Mr. Harry Chen (陈 喜), of Quanzhou Foreign Affairs, for accompanying me in Toy Ota (our van) on many of my jaunts around

Mr. Harry Chen
(Quanzhou FAO)

the countryside. He provided keen insights on the history and culture, invaluable books and literature, and unwavering moral support. Besides—I loved his turbocharged Beetle!

Thanks also to Miss Qu Weiwei (曲微微), of Quanzhou Overseas Chinese University's school of tourism, for her help in

researching various subjects, and for accompanying Harry and I on several trips.

Finally, heartfelt thanks to Mr. Wang Guoliang, of the Quanzhou Landscape Administration Office, for his invaluable assistance in so many ways—including providing nice accommodations in the Zaytun Hotel, which has become my home away from home.

Miss Qu Weiwei 曲微微

Enjoy Quanzhou!

Table of Contents

The Problem of China
Bertrand Russell (1922)[1]

"When I went to China, I went to teach; but every day that I stayed I thought less and less of what I had to teach them and more of what I had to learn from them. Among Europeans who lived a long time in China, I found this attitude not uncommon, but among those who stay is short, or who go only to make money, it is sadly rare. It is ratre because the Chinese do not excel in the things we really value—military prowess and industrial enterprise. But those who value wisdom or beauty, or even the simple enjoyment of life, will find more of these things in China than in the distracted and turbulent West, and will be happy to live where such things are valued. I wish I could hope that China, in return for our scientific knowledge, may give us something of her large tolerance and contemplative peace of mind....

"Should our lives be spent in building a mansion that we shall never have the leisure to inhabit?...

"The Chinese answer these questions in the negative, and therefore have to put up with poverty, disease and anarchy. But, to compensate for these evils, they have retained, as industrial nations have not, the capacity for civilized enjoyment, for leisure and laughter...The Chinese, of all classes, are more laughter-loving than any other race with which I am acquainted; they find amusement in everything, and a dispute can always be softened by a joke...

"The Chinese, from the highest to the lowest, have an imperturbable quiet dignity, which is usually not destroyed by a European education. They are not self-assertive, either individually or nationally; their pride is too profound for self-assertion. They admit China's military weakness...but they do not consider efficiency in homicide the most important quality in a man or a nation. I think that, at bottom, they think that China is the greatest nation in the world, and has the finest civilization."

---

[1] Bertrand Russell quoted from Cameron, 1997, p.400

Chapter 1
Introduction

"There is no people in the world wealthier than the Chinese"
Ibn Battuta[1] (Famed Arab Traveler, 1304-1358)

Introduction

Columbus may have ended up in a "New" World but what he really sought was an Ancient one. The admiral had devoured Marco Polo's accounts of the unimaginable wealth in China's Quanzhou, from which the Venetian vagabond sailed for home.

Columbus

Zaytun (the Arab name—a homonym for "olive," symbol of peace), was the largest port on earth, rivaling Alexandria in Egypt. Start of the Silk Road of the Sea, this was the legendary port of call for Ibn Battuta, Sinbad the Sailor, and Admiral Zheng He, who 70 years before Columbus sailed the seas in 440 foot treasure ships that would have dwarfed Columbus' little 85' Santa Maria.

Columbus Meets Zhenghe!

Columbus never made it to Zaytun, but I have! That mystic "City of Light" is just a 90 minute drive up the coast from my adopted home of Xiamen (which a few centuries ago was part of Quanzhou).

"At this city you must know is the Haven of Zaytun, frequented by all the ships of India, which bring thither spicery and all other kinds of costly wares. It is the port also that is frequented by all the merchants of Manzi, for hither is imported the most astonishing quantity of goods and of precious stones and pearls, and from this they are distributed all over Manzi. And I assure you that for one shipload of pepper that goes to Alexandria or elsewhere, destined for Christendom, there come a hundred such, aye and more too, to this haven of Zaytun; for it is one of the greatest havens in the world for commerce."

Marco Polo

Marco Polo (Venetian vagabond)

Zaytun's True Wealth   Marco Polo was impressed by Zaytun's gems, pearls, porcelain, and silk, but he overlooked the true wealth of this mythic port—the place and the people! Zaytun was blessed with an unparalleled natural wealth and beauty that the enlightened inhabitants maintained as meticulously as they crafted their miniature landscapes, which have been famous throughout Asia for 1000 years.

Zaytun was a city of gardens, lakes and forests, ringed by mountains, facing the sea, and nestled between two great rivers. Zaytun, with its three great concentric city walls, had a storybook setting that has inspired nearly 2,000 years of Chinese poets and philosophers.

Ancient Garden City

It is no wonder that the great Arab traveler Ibn Battuta remarked upon Quanzhou folks' love of gardens. The entire city was indeed like a miniature garden but on a gigantic scale, with each citizen playing their part—even as they to today.

5,015 Years of Balance For 1,000 years, Quanzhou folks have crafted their prize-winning miniature landscapes not to win prizes but for the sheer beauty of it. And even as they revel in the judicial juxtaposition of stone and miniature trees, so they have adapted their city to the confines of their unique topography to create not just family gardens but neighborhood gardens, public parks and city forests that reinforced rather than destroyed their environment. I suspect this uniquely Chinese sense of balance and long-term perspective explains how China has survived for 5,015 years (a Chinese professor told me China was 5,000 years old—and that was 15 years ago).

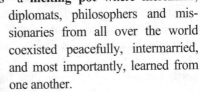

"Soup's Up!"

"Land is Life" is an old Chinese adage that proved true in Quanzhou. Both land and inhabitants thrived, and the City of Light became a global commercial and cultural crossroads—a **melting pot** where merchants, diplomats, philosophers and missionaries from all over the world coexisted peacefully, intermarried, and most importantly, learned from one another.

Ashab Mosque (1009 A.D.)

Jerusalem of Asia[2] UNESCO dubbed Quanzhou a "World Museum of Religion" because the city hosted every major religion, from Nestorian Christianity and Tibetan Buddhism to Islam. Quanzhou's Muslim community supposedly dates back to the day of Mohammed himself, and the Persian Manichean religion survives today only in Quanzhou. Quanzhou people not only did not lack diversity of religion or philosophy, they were also well grounded academically! Called the **Academy Upon the Sea**, Quanzhou produced 2,473 successful candidates in the highest imperial examinations, twenty prime ministers, and 950 nationally acclaimed scholars.

World Citizens   Broad exposure to world philosophies, religions and academics helped give Quanzhou people the uniquely global outlook that insured their prosperity both at home and abroad.   Today, over 5 million Overseas Chinese, and 40% of Taiwan's Han Chinese, trace their roots to Quanzhou. But Fujianese were a force to be reckoned with long before the City of Light became a beacon for the world.

The Fujian Flame   As we'll see in the next chapter when we visit China's best Maritime Museum, China's great maritime tradition was born right here in Fujian over 2,000 years ago when King Fuchai built a shipyard near Fuzhou.   From King Fuchai we get the name of our province, and the name for the great Fujian boats (fuchuan), with their "dragon eyes" painted on the prows so they could see where they were going—which too often was straight into the mouth of a watery hell.

Guang Sima claimed that during the 10th century, fully 40% to 50% of ships traveling from Fujian to North China were lost at sea! So it was with some awe that Koreans recorded the arrival of Quanzhou merchants as early as 1017 A.D.. They also visited Manchuria and Japan. Su Shi wrote, "Only the crafty merchants of Fujian dare to travel to Koryo where the kingdom urges them to seek profits. Men such as Xu Jian of Quanzhou are legion."   But if men such as Xu Jian were legion, it was partly because they had such little flat land back home to hang onto.

"8 parts mountain, 1 part water, 1 part field" (八山，一水，一分田) Fujian is blessed with everything but flat land. So much of Fujian is vertical that we could easily have the biggest province in China if someone flattened it. A millennium ago, Fujianese sought more farm land with massive land reclamation projects, but even after draining the malarial marshes and pushing back the sea, farm land was still inadequate, so the intrepid Fujianese took to commerce—and here they found their calling.

Fujianese Integrity Over the centuries, Fujianese developed a reputation not only for business prowess but also for unimpeachable integrity. In 1912, Reverend Pitcher wrote in "In and About Amoy":

"...what shall we say of them [Fujianese]? They are a part of a wonderful people...

"One hears all kinds of comment upon the deceptiveness of the Chinese and yet in business circles, the commercial world, they have the reputation of being the most straightforward and conscientious merchants in the whole Eastern hemisphere. This holds true here in Amoy...You may always depend upon the man with whom you may be dealing to deliver the goods. No matter how much they may lose in the transaction the Chinese have the reputation of fulfilling their contracts every time to the letter."

It was the people, as much as the place, which made Zaytun the natural start of the Silk Road of the Sea. And, of course, there was also Zaytun's silk...

"The first city which we reached after our sea voyage was the city of Zaytun... Zaytun is an immense city. In it are woven the damask silk and satin fabrics which go by its name, and which are superior to the fabrics of Khansa and Khan-Baliq. The port of Zaytun is one of the largest in the world, or perhaps the very largest. I saw in it about a hundred large junks; as for small junks, they could not be counted for multitude." Ibn Battuta, Arab Traveler (1304—1358)

Silk Road of the Sea "Silk Road" evokes images of deserts and camels, but the Maritime Silk Road accounted for much of the trade because one ship carried as much as 700 camels (and ships didn't spit at you). While Fujianese sailed the seven seas, the rest of the world sailed to Zaytun for tropical fruits, agricultural products, Chinese medicines--and Fujian's famous porcelain and silks (our English word 'satin' comes from "Zaytun").

Over 3,000 years ago, silk was worth its weight in gold in the West. The Roman poet Horace (65—8 B.C.) wrote about silk, and Lucan (39—65 A.D.) wrote of "Cleopatra's white breasts...revealed by the fabric... close-woven by the shuttle of the Seres [Chinese]."

The Secret of Silk   For centuries, Westerners beguiled by visions of Cleopatra's silky undies sought to discover silk's origin. Pliny (A.D.23—79), in *Natural History*, wrote that silk grew on trees!

"The first race encountered are the Seres, so famous for the fleecy product of their forests. This pale floss, which they find growing on the leaves, they wet with water, and then comb out, furnishing thus a double task to our womenkind in first dressing the threads, and then again of weaving them into silk fabrics. So has toil to be multiplied; so have the ends of the earth to be traversed: and all that a Roman dame may exhibit her charms in transparent gauze."

To safeguard silk's secret, China forbade the export of raw silk. Silk fabric was sent through Constantinople to the Island of Cos, where it was unweaved and used to produce Roman nobility's ethereal garments. Silk's secret was discovered only in 550 A.D., when Nestorian monks secreted silkworms in bamboo tubes and smuggled them out of China. But the production of porcelain was a tougher nut to crack.

Zaytun Porcelain   Even more desirable than Zaytun's silk was her porcelain. One of China's top porcelain centers, Quanzhou's delicate wares so bewitched Western rulers that some monarchs bankrupted national treasuries to amass their vast collections. (see page 209)

Fujian—Established Happiness   With silk, porcelain, and her other treasures, this province well deserved the name of "Fujian (福建, Fukien in old Romanization):"

"The name Fukien, which means 'established happiness,' in a large measure characterizes the people of this district. I think we may safely go further and say that this is true of the whole province. What we mean is this: they are not antagonistic to foreigners... With the exception of a few occasions, the Chinese in these parts have never exhibited any opposition to the stranger within their gates."
                    Pitcher, In and About Amoy, 1912, p.96

Unfortunately, that happiness was soon to be disestablished...

Rise and Fall   Zaytun was bustling by the early 7th century when Mohammed's two disciples arrived, followed closely by Nestorian Christians, Manicheans, and adherents of virtually every other religion and philosophy.   By the 13th century, Quanzhou was a magnificent city with three concentric walls encircling the central government area, inner city, and foreigner's quarters.

By Zheng He's day, China and India together accounted for over half of the world's gross national product (and Angus Madison, a British economic historian, claims China accounted for 29% of the globe's GNP as late as 1820!).   But within a century of Zheng He's day the legendary City of Light was extinguished.

Before his seventh voyage in 1432, Zheng He erected a tablet in Changle (near Fuzhou), in which he claimed to have "unified seas and continents" and "the countries beyond the horizons from the ends of the earth have all become subjects."   But his great expeditions had taken a heavy toll on the land—especially on the common folk, who received nothing in return for their sacrifices to build the fleets.

While Westerners made a killing at commerce (Magellan's crew once sold 26 tons of cloves for 10,000 times the cost!), the Emperor's fleet was built primarily to impress the world with the glories of China (and, of course, her Emperor). And the ships returned not with practical commodities but cargoes of exotic gifts and luxuries for the imperial court (primarily the corrupt eunuchs).

The Emperor decried the waste, saying, "I do not care for foreign things. I accept them because they come from far away and show the sincerity of distant peoples, but we should not celebrate this." His sentiments echoed those of Chinese 1500 years earlier, whom Pliny wrote were,
> "inoffensive in their manners indeed; but, like the beasts of the forest, they eschew the contact of mankind; and, though ready to engage in trade, wait for it to come to them instead of seeking it out."

Dousing the City of Light   Not long after Zheng He's death, China closed her doors and destroyed the greatest navy the world had ever seen. Whereas the Ming navy had 3,500 ships in the early 1400s, within decades it was a capital offense to build boats with more than two masts.

In 1525, the emperor ordered the destruction of all seafaring ships, and the arrest of the merchants who sailed them. By 1551, it was a crime to sail the seas in a ship with more than one mast.

Rekindling the City of Light   Zaytun had so captured the imagination of foreigners that some thought it was China's capital! In 1515, Giovanni d'Empoli wrote, "The Grand Can is the King of China, and he dwells at Zeiton." Trade ceased, the ports silted up, and that mystic City of Light was snuffed out, but thanks to a couple of decades of dramatic reform and opening up, Quanzhou's new generation is as excited about their future as they are proud of their past, and Quanzhou is becoming once again a global commercial and cultural crossroads.

#3! Quanzhou people still have their age-old knack for business! Over the past decade, this resurrected city's annual GDP grew an average of 26%—#3 amongst China's top 212 cities! And Quanzhou is using this newfound wealth to make the place a better place to live.

Return to the Garden City
Quanzhou people are once again managing their city with the same meticulous care as they lavish upon their gardens and miniature landscapes. And Quanzhou gardening is grassroots, not a top down affair begun by bureaucrats spouting "One earth" slogans. For example, from 1998 to 2002,

Quanzhou youth spent 1.3 million man hours (including girl hours) planting over 6 million trees.

From family gardens to neighborhood gardens, city parks, forests, and lakes, Quanzhou people are again molding their city to their unique environment, rather than wrecking that environment to accommodate urban sprawl.

The Wall   Quanzhou, once famous for its city walls, now has a new wall that proves the people are more forward thinking and pragmatic than ever. This 1 billion Yuan project, with its grand battlements, towers and gates, recaptures the feel of old Zaytun—but it has many immensely practical uses. The wall shields the city from floods, offers beautiful roadside gardens and forests for recreation, and the parallel ring road deflects traffic around the city and lessens congestion and pollution. Even the wall's interior is put to use. The endless row of rooms will be rented out to accommodate Quanzhou folks' entrepreneurial bent as they are used for shops, work areas, cafes.

Endless Cultural Traditions   Quanzhou is also resurrecting and breathing new life into its endless number of cultural sites and traditions. This ancient city of traders, educators, philosophers, and adherents of virtually all major religions, also gave birth to Chinese marionettes, S. Shaolin Kung fu, and Southern Chinese music and opera. Quanzhou produced the prized blanc' de Chine porcelain now displayed proudly in museums around the world. Hui'an's 1700 year tradition of stonework attracts admirers and buyers from all over the planet.

夏榮峰

Mr. Xia, Puppet Master
Amoymagic.com

Dozens of architectural relics include one of Islam's top ten mosques, the last temple to the Persian Mani, and engineering marvels like the ancient Luoyang and Anping stone bridges (longest in the world). Quanzhou is also famous for its unique cuisines, and, of course, the Anxi tea that sparked the Boston Tea Party.

Above ground, not below Some experts claim that modern Quanzhou has more archaeological artifacts than any Chinese city but Beijing or Xi'an, [3] but as Quanzhou people quickly point out, "Xi'an's heritage is below ground—ours is above!" And so are her hopes for the future...

Amoymagic.com   S. Shaolin Kung Fu

Touring Zaytun – a Sample Itinerary

An official Quanzhou brochure boasts "2,000 tourist sites famous at home and abroad," so where on earth (or China) do you start? With a few dozen trips to Quanzhou under my belt (eat your heart out, Columbus!), I suggest the following simple itinerary.   For updates, or to share your own discoveries, check out my wife Susan Marie's website,   **http://www.Amoymagic.com.**

1.   Maritime Museum   The first stop in Zaytun should be the UNESCO-sponsored Maritime Museum—China's biggest and best! After enjoying these eye-opening bilingual exhibits you'll have a better handle on not only ancient China's marvelous maritime achievements but also ancient Quanzhou's pivotal role in both domestic and international affairs. And after the museum, head downtown.

2.   Zhongshan Rd. Historic District, was so abuzz with activity 1,000 years ago that one visitor said it was "intoxicating." Treasure Street had more gems, jewels, and gold than any place on the planet (today, the best buy is a granny's great sausages-on-a-stick).

The Zhongshan Road restoration and preservation project was awarded the "Excellent Relic Protection in Asian-Pacific Area" in UNESCO's Relic Protection Campaign. After a stroll along this delightfully shaded street, enjoy a dozen major sites all within walking distance (or catch a pedicab if you can wake the operator). With a good 3 dozen tours of Quanzhou under my belt (and excellent Quanzhou cuisine hanging over it!), I suggest this simple itinerary:

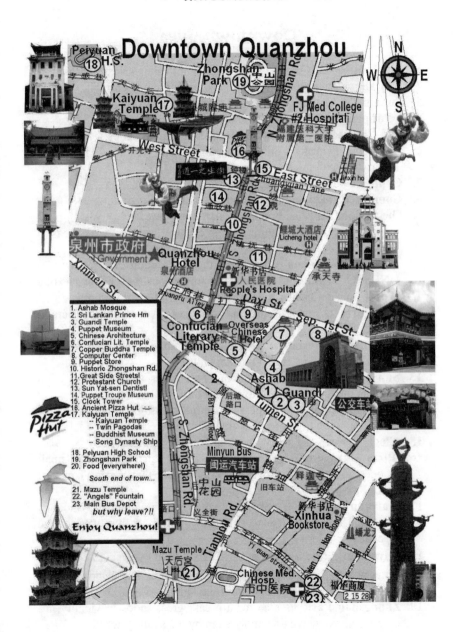

Downtown Quanzhou

Peiyuan (18) H.S.

Zhongshan Park (19) 中山公园

Kaiyuan Temple (17)

FJ Med College #2 Hospital
福建医科大学附属第二医院

West Street (16)

East Street (15)
(13)
(14)
(12)
(10)
(11)

泉州市政府
★ Quanzhou Hotel
Government

Xinmen St.

People's Hospital
Daxi St.

Sep. 1st St.

Confucian Literary Temple
(6)   Overseas Chinese Hotel
(5)   (7)   (8)

(4)
Ashab   Guandi
(1)
(2) (3)

Tumen St.

公交车站

1. Ashab Mosque
2. Sri Lankan Prince Hm
3. Guandi Temple
4. Puppet Museum
5. Chinese Architecture
6. Confucian Lit. Temple
7. Copper Buddha Temple
8. Computer Center
9. Puppet Store
10. Historic Zhongshan Rd.
11. Great Side Streets!
12. Protestant Church
13. Sun Yat-sen Dentist!
14. Puppet Troupe Museum
15. Clock Tower
16. Ancient Pizza Hut
17. Kaiyuan Temple
    -- Kaiyuan Temple
    -- Twin Pagodas
    -- Buddhist Museum
    -- Song Dynasty Ship
18. Peiyuan High School
19. Zhongshan Park
20. Food (everywhere!)

    South end of town...

21. Mazu Temple
22. "Angels" Fountain
23. Main Bus Depot
    but why leave?!!

Enjoy Quanzhou!

Pizza Hut

Minyun Bus
闽运汽车站

S. Zhongshan Rd.

Tianhou Rd.

Xinhua Bookstore
新华书店

Mazu Temple
天后宫 (21)

Chinese Med. Hosp.
市中医院 (22)
(23)

Downtown Sites

1. **Ashab Mosque**. One of Islam's top 10 holy sites. Next door is...
2. **Sri Lankan Prince's** home, tourist shopping mall behind it.
3. **Guandi Temple** adjoins the Sri Lankan Prince's home.
4. **A Puppet Museum** is right behind Ashab Mosque.
5. **Old Chinese Architecture** beautifully rebuilt as shops.
6. **Confucius Temple** is only a ten minute walk west of Ashab. Nice literary museum.
7. **Copper Buddha Temple**, park, lake and pavilion
8. **Computer Plaza** around the corner from Copper Buddha
9. **The Puppet Store** and puppet makers just past KFC. Watch puppets being carved, costumes being embroidered, in work areas in back.
10. **At Historic Zhongshan Rd**—the restoration project won a UNESCO award! As you stroll, sample local snacks, and exotic West China delicacies pedaled by Xinjiang Muslim vendors.
11. **Side Streets** lead to hidden treasures like ancient officials' homes.
12. **Quannan Protestant Church** (new church under construction). Quanzhou has over 170 Protestant churches!
13. **Sun Yat-sen** left an inscription in, of all places, a dentist office! It's near the intersection clock tower, on the left.
14. **Quanzhou Puppet Troupe's Museum** is absolutely incredible—a **must-see** second only to Maritime Museum.
15. **Clock Tower** – a Timely Landmark to get your bearings
16. **Pizza Hut** patrons vie to build the tallest salad possible in small wooden bowls. Some tower precariously like the Leaning Tower of Pizza.
17. **Kaiyuan Temple Complex** (includes Twin Pagodas, Buddhist Museum, and Song Dynasty Ship Exhibition) is just west of the clock tower.
18. **Peiyuan High School** (培元中学), started 100 years ago by a missionary with the London Presbyterian Mission, has inscriptions by Sun Yat-sen and his wife Soong Ling Qing.
19. **Zhongshan Park** is nice for a break; great shops in vicinity, including an extensive art supply shop by the south gate.

20. **Food!**   I moved to China primarily because Chinese food is too expensive in America—and Quanzhou cuisine fits the bill perfectly! Review the chapter on Quanzhou Cuisine, then try any of the hundreds of fine restaurants, or try out the "Delicacy Street" just east of the puppet store about a 15 minute walk.

In the south of town...

21. **Mazu Temple**, to the very south of town.
22. **Quanzhou Angel sculpture**/dancing fountain in intersection by 23.
23. **Quanzhou Main Bus Station**

City Outskirts

1. **Muslim Holy Tombs** (just east of the Maritime Museum)
2. **Overseas Chinese Museum**. Most Overseas Chinese are from Fujian, and most of them from Quanzhou, hence the museum.
3. **Qingyuan Mountain** to the north (many sites, including China's largest Taoist statues, and carvings of the three Tibetan lamas)
4. **S. Shaolin Temple** – home of Southern Shaolin Kung Fu, the young abbot, Master Shi, is putting Quanzhou's martial arts back on the map.
5. **Luoyang Bridge**, one of my favorite sites, is just to the north.
6. **Jiuri Mountain**, official start of the Silk Road, is a few kilometers west of the city.
7. **Stone Bamboo Shoot**—this tall, slim stone was a totem for fertility worship, and ...well, we'll leave that one for later!
8. **Wenling Delicacy Street**—a lane dedicated to fine local cuisine.
9. **Parks and Gardens.** Quanzhou has many beautiful parks and gardens. Also note the famous miniature landscapes.
10. **Well**... explore for yourself, and e-mail us your discoveries!

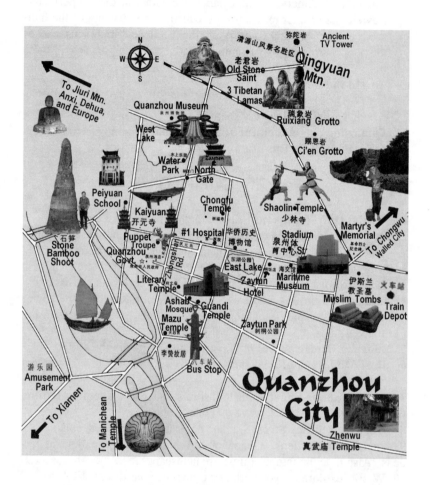

Ancient
TV Tower

弥陀岩

清源山风景名胜区

老君岩
Old Stone
Saint

Qingyuan
Mtn.

3 Tibetan
Lamas

To Jiuri Mtn.
Anxi, Dehua,
and Europe

Quanzhou Museum

泉州博物馆

瑞象岩
Ruixiang Grotto

West
Lake

赐恩岩
Ci'en Grotto

水上乐园
Water
Park

North
Gate

Peiyuan
School

Chongfu
Temple
崇福寺

Shaolin Temple
少林寺

石笋
Stone
Bamboo
Shoot

Kaiyuan
开元寺

#1 Hospital
第一医院

华侨历史
博物馆

Stadium
泉州体
育中心 St.

Martyr's
Memorial
革命烈士
纪念碑

To Chongwu
Walled City

Puppet
Troupe
Quanzhou
Gov't.
泉州酒店
☆ 泉州市人民政府

Zhongshan Rd.

状元酒店

东湖公园

East Lake
Zaytun
Hotel

梅园酒店

Maritime
Museum
海交馆

伊斯兰
教圣墓
Muslim Tombs

火车站

Train
Depot

Literary
Temple

Ashab
Mosque
Mazu
Temple

Guandi
Temple

Zaytun Park
刺桐公园

李贽故居

汽车站
Bus Stop

Quanzhou
City

游乐园
Amusement
Park

To Xiamen

To Manichean Temple

Zhenwu
真武庙 Temple

Hit the Road!

After Quanzhou City, we'll head for Quanzhou's counties of:

1. **Hui'an** (ancient walled city, Hui'an girls, extraterrestrial beaches, and China's best stone masons)
2. **Nan' an** (birthplace of Koxinga, Cai's Minnan Village, and Anping Bridge—our planet's longest stone bridge)
3. **Jinjiang** (our planet's last Manichaean temple, Muslim Ancestral Hall of Chendai, ancient kilns)
4. **Anxi** (home of the tea that sparked the Boston Tea Party)
5. **Dehua** (ancient porcelain center, and origin of the blanc de chine porcelain coveted by collectors and museums worldwide)
6. **Yongchun** (incense capital, and dongguan bridge)
7. **Shishi** (garment capital of China, Sisters-in-law tower, and China's largest ocean theme park).

Whether ancient Zaytun or modern Quanzhou, there's plenty to see, but to appreciate both, start your visit with China's best Maritime Museum.

**Problems "steering"?
At least he's not hitting the horn.**

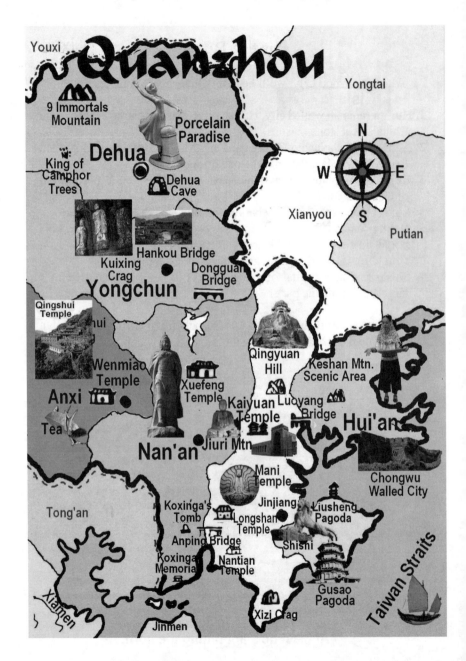

Youxi

Quanzhou

Yongtai

9 Immortals
Mountain

Porcelain
Paradise

King of
Camphor
Trees

Dehua

Dehua
Cave

Xianyou

Putian

Hankou Bridge

Kuixing
Crag

Dongguan
Bridge

Yongchun

Qingshui
Temple

hui

Qingyuan
Hill

Keshan Mtn.
Scenic Area

Wenmiao
Temple

Xuefeng
Temple

Kaiyuan
Temple

Luoyang
Bridge

Anxi

Tea

Jiuri Mtn

Hui'an

Nan'an

Mani
Temple

Chongwu
Walled City

Tong'an

Koxinga's
Tomb

Jinjiang

Liusheng
Pagoda

Longshan
Temple

Anping Bridge

Shishi

Koxinga
Memorial

Nantian
Temple

Xiamen

Gusao
Pagoda

Jinmen

Xizi Crag

Taiwan Straits

Supplement

On The City and Great Haven of Zaytun
By Marco Polo

(Yule-Cordier Edition, Volume II, 1903 edition,
and 1920 addenda)

"Now when you quit Fuju and cross the River, you travel for five days south-east through a fine country, meeting with a constant succession of flourishing cities, towns, and villages, rich in every product. You travel by mountains and valleys and plains, and in some places by great forests in which are many of the trees which give Camphor. There is plenty of game on the road, both of bird and beast. The people are all traders and craftsmen of Fuju. When you have accomplished those five days journey you arrive at the very great and noble city of ZAYTUN, which is also subject to Fuju.

"At this city you must know is the Haven of Zaytun, frequented by all the ships of India, which bring thither spicery and all other kinds of costly wares. It is the port also that is frequented by all the merchants of Manzi, for hither is imported the most astonishing quantity of goods and of precious stones and pearls, and from this they are distributed all over Manzi. And I assure you that for one shipload of pepper that goes to Alexandria or elsewhere, destined for Christendom, there come a hundred such, aye and more too, to this haven of Zaytun; for it is one of the greatest havens in the world for commerce.

"The Great Kaan derives a very large revenue from the duties paid in this city and haven; for you must know that on all the merchandise imported, including precious stones and pearls, he levies a duty of ten per cent, or in other words takes tithe of everything. Then again the ship's charge for freight on small wares is 30 per cent, on pepper 44 per cent, and on lignaloes, sandalwood, and other bulky goods 40 per cent, so that between freight and the Kaan's duties the merchant has to pay a good half the value of his investment [though on the other half he makes such a profit that he is always glad to come back with a new supply of merchandize]. But you may well believe from what I have said that the Kaan hath a vast revenue from this city.

"There is a great abundance here of all provision for every necessity of man's life. [It is a charming country, and the people are very quiet, and fond of an easy life. Many come hither from Upper India to have their bodies painted with the needle in the way we have elsewhere described, there being many adepts at this craft in the city.]

"Let me tell you, and also that in this province there is a town called TYUNJU where they make vessels of porcelain of all sizes, the finest that can be imagined. They make it nowhere but in that city, and thence it is exported all over the world. Here it is abundant and very cheap, insomuch that for a Venice groat you can buy three dishes so fine that you could not imagine better.

"I should tell you that in this city (i.e. of Zaytun) they have a peculiar language. [For you must know that throughout all Manzi they employ one speech and one kind of writing only, but yet there are local differences of dialect, as you might say of Genoese, Milanese, Florenties, and Neapolitans, who though they speak different dialects can understand one another.]

"And I assure you that the Great Kaan has as large customs and revenues from this kingdom of Chonka [Fujian?] as from Kinsay, aye and more too.

"We have now spoken of but three out of the nine kingdoms of Manzi, to wit Yanju and Kinsay and Fuju. We could tell you about the other six, but it would be too long a business; so we will say no more about them.

"And now you have heard all the truth about Cathay and Manzi and many other countries, as has been set down in this book...."

Endnotes

[1] Ibn Battuta was born in Tangier on 24th February, 1304, and after a stay in India was dispatched by the Sultan Muhammad Thugluq to China. After many adventures, he returned home in 1349, having traveled, according to Yule's estimate, over 75,000 miles by land and sea. "The Traveler of Islam" died twenty years later—but fortunately not before dictating his travels (which many disbelieved at the time) to a royal secretary, Ibn Juzayyat Fes.

[2] Jerusalem of Asia: Arabs called Quanzhou "Zaytun," and Jerusalem "Zaytuniyah"

[3] "Learning About Quanzhou; the Archaeology of a Medieval Port in Fujian, China." Richard Pearson, Li Min, and Li Guo, Department of Anthropology and Sociology, University of British Columbia

Chapter 2

Quanzhou Maritime Museum
海外交通历史博物馆

The sign in the foyer of Quanzhou's UNESCO sponsored maritime museum (China's best!) sums up well Quanzhou folks' aspirations: "UNESCO, Peace and Friendship, Cultural Dialogue, Looking Back on the Past, Looking Forward to the Future."

Quanzhou Maritime Museum

The more I look back on the past, the more I appreciate that the Chinese were a peaceful people (at least outside their own borders). Had Chinese been more inclined to conquering than commerce, they could have easily dominated our planet 1,000 years ago, and today the world would be wielding chopsticks at McRice outlets.

A millennium ago, China had a vast navy armed to the teeth with weapons the West had never imagined. They had cannon, giant crossbows, and even land and sea mines.

Advanced shipbuilding features like watertight compartments weren't used by Westerners until the mid-1800s! And even 2,000 years ago they had battleships with paddlewheels that could just about walk right up onto land! China's shipbuilding

Paddlewheel Battleship

greatness continued right into the 19th century...

"In February, 1822, Captain Pearl, of the English ship Indiana, coming through Gaspar Straits, fell in with the cargo and crew of a wrecked junk, and saved 198 persons out of 1600, with whom she had left Amoy, whom he landed at Pontianak." [1]

Imagine a junk, almost 200 years ago, with 1600 passengers! Yet even that ship was dwarfed by the treasure ships of Zheng He's day, as you'll learn in Quanzhou's Maritime Museum. Famous Arab traveler Ibn Battuta described the magnificent "Zaytun Ships":

Zaytun Ships

"The large ships have anything from twelve down to three sails, which are made of bamboo rods plaited like mats. A ship carries a complement of a thousand men, six hundred of whom are sailors and four hundred men-at-arms, including archers, men with shields and arbalists, who throw naphtha [flaming petroleum]. These vessels are built **only in the towns of Zaytun** [Quanzhou] and Sin-Kalan [Guangzhou]. The vessel has four decks and contains rooms, cabins, and saloons for merchants; a cabin has chambers and a lavatory, and can be locked by its occupant, who takes along with him slave girls and wives. Often a man will live in his cabin unknown to any of the others on board until they meet on reaching some town... Some of the Chinese own large numbers of ships on which their factors are sent to foreign countries."

Ibn Battuta

The World of China's Ships   The second floor, to the right, recounts the history of shipbuilding, beginning with a video of how the ancients discovered flotation (hollow gourds tied to their waists) and went on to bamboo rafts, dugout canoes, animal hide coracles (Tibet), boats, and large ships. I was surprised to see a 2,000-year-old drawing of a Dragon Boat Race (2,000 years, and they haven't beat the dragon yet).

Stealth Junk? I showed some guests the epitome of ancient China's maritime hi-tech. When they complained it was just an empty glass case, I said, "See how well it works!"

"Stealth Junk"
Ancient hi-tech

Yakskin Coracle -- a holey boat for holymen?

Tibetan yak skin coracle was nothing to yak about, but to its left was a beautifully painted canoe used by natives of a small island off Taiwan's east coast; it reminded me of ceremonial Native American canoes.

Getting my goat. My friends thought I was kidding when I told them Chinese made rafts from inflated sheepskins. A photo on the wall behind the model shows a gigantic river raft made of over 700 sheepskins!

B.B.
Blowing Up the Raft!

Dr. Bill on the Yellow River

Miniature Boat Models A vast array of intricately detailed boat models show the sheer diversity and sophistication of Chinese ship building. Boats were designed according to use, climate, and water conditions (rough or

偏头船 (明、清)
又名歪头船，航行于荣成地区水域。
Crooked-bow boat (Ming/Qing, model)
Plying the waters of the Rongcheng region.

smooth seas, hot or cold climes). My favorite is the crooked bow boat. I've no idea why a ship would be designed with a crooked bow. I asked if it was used by crooked bureaucrats on vacation but that didn't go over very well.

Grand Houseboats, owned by foreigners and wealthy Chinese, used to ply Fujian's rivers during the hot summers. As I write this in a sweltering Amoy July, I wish I was on one!

Chinese Houseboat

Fujian Fishing Boats

Tying the Knot!   The museum used to have an excellent knot-tying station but it was removed. Maybe too many lasses were tying the knot.   Months later, someone made a half-hearted attempt to resurrect the exhibit by dangling a few frayed bits of rope on a pole, and hanging a few nicely framed knots on other walls, but unlike the previous exhibit, there were no instructions, so it proved to be a knotty problem for Jim, who was soon at the end of his rope. He should have been more resourceful, like the string.[1]

Tying the knot!

At the end of his rope!

South Pointing Needles

Compass   Another display showed various Chinese "South Pointing Needles"—the Chinese name for compass. They would, of course, say compasses point south and not north—on pure principal. But since Chinese invented compasses (and just about everything else), I suppose they've a right to call it what they want.   We Westerners were so ignorant of compasses that when they finally came into use in Europe, captains forbade sailors from eating onions lest they interfere with the cunning device's powers!

"A gift for European traders!"

---

[1] The bartender kicked out a string, saying, "This is a 'rope only' bar." The resourceful string simply unraveled one end, tied himself in a knot, and reentered the bar. The bartender demanded, "Aren't you the same string I just kicked out?" The string replied, "I'm a frayed knot."

Koxinga, the pirate-cum-patriot born in Japan of a Japanese mother and Quanzhou Chinese father, was well represented with paintings, ship models, clips from the Koxinga TV series (I played the last Dutch governor of Taiwan!), and a diorama with lights, sound and action, of the great battle in which he wrested control of Taiwan from the "greedy grasp of the Dutch invaders."

Koxinga--the hero who got Taiwan out of Dutch

Flagging Exhibit   For the record, however, the two Dutch ships' are flying French flags, not Dutch flags! Both nation's flags do have red, white and blue stripes, but the Dutch stripes are horizontal, while the French stripes are vertical.   Though perhaps such details are too trivial to matter…

I mentioned the flag issue several times to the museum staff. One finally said, "Dutch, French—six of one and half dozen of the other.[2] They're both foreign." She paused, then added for good measure, "Koxinga fought them 300

Koxinga fights the Dutch, or French, or -- whatever

years ago. Maybe the Dutch and French have switched flags by now." Good point.

---

[2] 半斤八两 (banjin baliang)—half a jin (1.1 lbs.) or 8 ounces. A Chinese jin used to be sixteen ounces; nowadays it's ten, but they still use the same expression.

Standard Issue
Pot-bellied
Laoban
(Boss)

Dioramas & Displays The East side of the museum's upper floor has delightful dioramas detailing the construction of wooden ships, which hasn't changed much in centuries. Dozens of models of fishing junks, treasure ships and warships help convey the complexity of ancient Chinese ship making. The sails were so stable that during the past decade many designers have begun to adapt them to Western yachts and sailing ships.

Thanks to innovative ships, navigational techniques, mastery of mapmaking, and the compass, Chinese seafarers like Admiral Zheng He sailed pretty much around the globe. In fact, Gavin Menzie, former submarine commander in the British Navy, claims that Zheng He's fleet, not Columbus, discovered America. While some claims appear, to me at least, a bit farfetched, his book, 1421 —*The Year China Discovered America*, has at least gotten Westerners' attention.

Admiral Zheng He, 1421
(Adapted from *Amoy Magic*)

The eunuch admiral and his female admirers

Zheng He, China's most illustrious adventurer, was a Muslim descendant of the King of Bukhara (southern Uzbekistan), and the governor of Yunnan, who was the last Mongol to hold out against the Ming. After the Ming defeated Yunnan in 1381, they castrated thousands of youth, including Zheng He—a cruel punishment for a Muslim boy dreaming of adulthood and four wives. But Zheng He proved to be an excellent scholar and linguist, and his skills in court (if not courting) got the attention of the prince who overthrew the emperor, and made Zheng He an admiral.

85 feet vs. over 400 feet!

Columbus' Santa Maria vs. Zheng He's ship

Over his 28-year career, Zheng He commanded at least 317 ships and 37,000 men. He sailed from Korea to Antarctica and around Africa into the Atlantic. His navigational charts remained unsurpassed for centuries (though his geographical knowledge was not perfect; Zheng He wrote that both Christ and Mohammed were from Western India, which he assumed included all of the Middle East).

During his first voyage, in 1405, Zheng He commanded 62 ships and 27,800 men. The first voyage passed peaceably enough, but during the second voyage of 1409, Zheng He had differences with the King of Ceylon and hauled him back to China. Even today, a Sri Lankan prince's home stands to the east of Quanzhou's Ashab Mosque (adjoining the ancient temple).

Alas, Zheng He's 7th voyage was his last. The Emperor decided that the rest of the world had nothing China needed, and after Zheng He died, international trade declined as well. Decades later, all records of Zheng He's exploits were destroyed, Chinese were forbidden to travel abroad, and the members of Zaytun's Islamic community, facing increasing persecution, adopted Chinese surnames and melded right into Han society—so well, in fact, that in the 1990s some Hui had no idea their ancestors were Middle Eastern Arabs until researchers informed them.

It's no wonder that UNESCO calls Quanzhou a World Museum of Religion. Today, tens of thousands of Quanzhou people are descended from Zaytun's early foreign settlers, and they brought with them not only Islam but every other religion imaginable, as we shall see in the museum's fascinating collection of foreign religious artifacts.

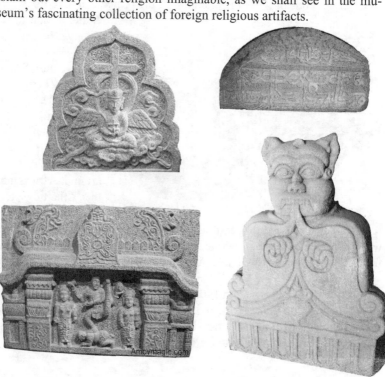

Quanzhou
A UNESCO World Museum of Religion

The foreigners who flocked to ancient Zaytun exchanged not just commodities but cultures, philosophies, and religions.

The Maritime Museum's hundreds of ancient religious relics help us realize that, at one time, Zaytun was indeed the "Jerusalem of Asia," with representatives of every religion imaginable.

The ground floor hall to the left of the foyer displays religious artifacts unearthed over recent decades. There are so many, in fact, that they are even scattered about the field behind the museum (hence the present construction of the large Islamic Heritage Center).

Amoymagic.com
Over 150 Islamic relics

Over 150 Islamic tombstones and carved stone fragments were recovered during the dismantling of the city walls during the first part of the 20th century. While most were from cities scattered across Persia, some were from Yemen, Hamdan, and al

Amoymagic.com

Malf in Turkestan, and Khalat in Armenia.

The Arab Connection

China's rulers valued Muslims' business skills so highly that they appointed them to high municipal and provincial level posts. Mr. Pu Chongqing (蒲重庆), who runs an incense factory in Yongchun (永春) and is a descendant of Muslims who came to Quanzhou about 1200 A.D., said one of his ancestors was Pu Shougen (蒲寿更), the Quanzhou Maritime Commis-

Persian ship (painted 1240 a.d.)

sioner, and later assistant to the governor. Another ancestor was governor of Chongqing in Sichuan, in W. China. But foreigners' power went to their heads and when they tried to take charge, the incensed Han Chinese put them in their place, and many hightailed it to some other place.

Muslim Chinese   Muslims are still in Zaytun, but they've blended into the woodwork. After their failed coup, Zaytun's Laowai avoided trouble with increasingly xenophobic Chinese neighbors by adopting Chinese names. Baiqi Island now has over 10,000 descendants of Arabs, all sur-named Guo. They did not even know they had Arab blood until historians told them recently, and the Bu and Huang people of Yunlu Village learned that they were descendants of Pu Shougeng, the ancient Arab customs officer.

Triangles and Calculators   Muslims also traded in knowledge. Much of Western science and mathematics we owe to Arab traders who sailed from ancient Zaytun with storehouses of mathematical and scientific knowledge more precious than their cargoes of silk, porcelain and pearls.

Pascal's triangle, for instance, was not invented by the great French philosopher Blaise Pascal (1623-1662) but by Chinese centuries earlier. Pascal is also credited with inventing the adding machine, but centuries earlier Chinese had been ciphering with the abacus, which in the hands of a Chinese merchant or tax collector was deadly accurate. (I've never understood the devilish device, which some say was invented in ancient Persia. I'm not surprised. Who but Saddam's ancestors would have dared?)

The museum's barely legible Muslim relics are in Chinese and Arabic. The Arabic often has quotes from the Koran, or poetry, but the Chinese translations are much more straightforward—like "Dead Foreigner."

A Yuan Dynasty stone quotes the Koran in Arabic but in Chinese simply reads, "General Kang died on 1st day of the 4th month." (April 1st?!)

Side 1: Koran 55:26, and
"Death is a cup from which all men drink." (Sufi poem)
Side 2: Koran 9:21-22

My favorites include a stone found outside the southwest city gate in 1978. It reads, "The arrow of death has hit!" Another stone, excavated from the South City gate in 1946, has quotes from the Koran (9:21-22 and 55:26), and a Sufi poem, "Death is a cup from which all men drink."

Should have boiled the water first.

Christian Artifacts   The museum has more than 40 Christian relics, with nearly 1,000 lines of inscriptions—the largest collection of its kind. Many of the Yuan Dynasty headstones were unearthed from the wall foundation of the east gate in 1947. The languages include Chinese, Latin, Syro-Turkic (Turkish writtten in Syriac script), and even the unusual Phags-pa (script based on Tibetan and Chinese).

Syrian inscription: On the earth under the Holy Father in the name of the Holy Father and Holy Son.
Chinese inscription on the reverse side

One wonders how Tibet fit into all this.

Christian inscription in
Phags-pa (Tibetan/Chinese)

Quanzhou discovered that its heritage included Tibetan Buddhism when the outer layer
of three "Buddhist" monks on Qingyuan
Mountain was removed to discover that, underneath, they were Tibetan lamas!   Perhaps
Nestorians and Tibetans arrived together!

Nestorians were a millennium ahead of their
time.   Their advanced medical skills opened
doors everywhere, and wherever they went they
established language centers and translated their
scriptures into the local tongues.

Nestorians had missions in Tibet, and
some historians believe the Tibetans actually adapted their rites for worshipping the
dead from Nestorian practices (who expanded upon ancestor worship to please an
Emperor anxious to please his extinguished
forebears).   Nestorian syncretism (which
in the end proved their doom, not their salvation) is seen in the tombstones with a
four-winged angel beneath the Christian cross
in a Buddhist lotus position before a lotus.

Nestorian Tombstone

At one time, hundreds of thousands of Nestorians were scattered
throughout China, and a Nestorian metropolitan set up a center right here
in Zaytun.   And then the Nestorians vanished almost without a trace.
Some tombstones are of Franciscan Catholics, like Bishop Antonius, or
Bishop Bar Solomon, who died in 1313.   I was amazed at how far afield
Franciscans roamed within a mere century of Francis' death, and after
reading so much about the 3rd Franciscan Bishop of Zaytun, Andrew of
Perugia (who supervised construction of the Franciscan Cathedral out-
side of the East Gate), I was excited to see his headstone on display.
Though I did wonder where the Bishop now rests his head.

Andrew's headstone was unearthed in 1946 at the foundation of the
city wall, near the Dragon Temple.   The Latin inscription reads, "Here
lies at rest the Catholic priest Andrew of Perugia, follower of Jesus
Christ."

Hindu Relics The Maritime Museum displays some of the 300+ Hindu architectural and sculptural fragments discovered in Quanzhou. Many were found in the vicinity of the Tonghuai Gate, indicating there was probably a Hindu temple in the southeastern part of the city.

In 1933, an elephant presenting a lotus to Shiva lingam was discovered in a small temple on Xianlei street. In 1934, workers at the drill grounds excavated the 4-armed Protector of Hinduism, with

Over 300 Hindu stone fragments...

upper two arms holding the chakra and sangra. Even the ancient Kaiyuan Buddhist temple has a couple of Hindu columns added during reconstruction. Hinduism was strong in Quanzhou because of the close ties between Quanzhou merchants and Tamil guilds in India.

Manichaean Relics The last section of the religious relics display is devoted to Persian's Manicheanism. A legend beside some strange dog-like carvings say they resemble Assyrian art, so I'm guessing they are Manichaean. The carved granite Buddha-like Mani, by the way, is a reproduction of the real McCoy (or real McMani?) in in our planet's last Mani temple (southeast of the city in Jinjiang.

Inscribed with Manichean Scriptures
(found in Hanjiang, Putian)

Quanzhou's Sole Jewish Relic?

On October 10th, 2001, Xinhua News Agency reported that workers had unearthed from beneath the ancient Deji Gate what may be the first archaeological proof of the ancient Jewish community. Jews weren't the first to use a six-pointed star (Hindus also use it, with the Tamil "Om" in the center). But an excavated synagogue in Roman era Capernaum had a "Star of David" architectural motif, so

Ancient "Star of David?"
(unearthed in Quanzhou)

the Quanzhou stone may prove to be of Jewish origin as well—if it survives the elements. [After months of searching, I finally found it lying unprotected in the open courtyard of the Mazu Tianfei Temple].[3]

That Zaytun had a large Jewish community is confirmed by many sources, from Arab traders to Bishop Andrew of Perugia, who in January, 1326, lamented in a letter that Zaytun's Jews obstinately refused to undergo Christian baptism.

In the controversial book *City of Light*, which purports to be a translation of the journal of a Jewish traveler who reached Zaytun before Marco Polo, Jacob d'Ancona wrote that Zaytun had 2,000 Jews, and many tens of thousands were scattered around the rest of China, their ancestors having arrived during the days of the patriarchs. Some say that the Lost Tribes of Israel are in China! Though given the maps they use here, I can see how they got lost.

In the next chapter we'll visit sites in the UNESCO award-winning downtown area—and I'll even give you a map so you don't end up with the Lost Tribes!

---

[3] Reach Tianfei temple on #24 bus or special tourist bus #601. Hours: 8:00 to 17:30 Phone: 220-3731

Supplement

Zaytun's Openness to Foreign Religions

"As for the doctrine of the Occident which exalts I'ien Chiu [天主, Lord of Heaven—Christian God], it is … contrary to the orthodoxy [of China's Classics], and it is only because Christians are thoroughly versed in mathematical sciences that the State uses them. Beware, lest you forget that."

Emperor Kangxi

"Passing through many cities and towns, I came to a certain noble city which is called Zaytun, where we Friars Minor have two Houses…The city is twice as great as Bologna, and in it are many monasteries of devotees, idol-worshippers every man of them. In one of those monasteries which I visited there were 3,000 monks.. The place is one of the best in the world

Friar Odoric[2] (in China from 1323-1327)

All but one of Zaytun's 7 mosques have vanished, and Ashab is but a shell of its former grandeur—but Christians don't even have a shell left standing. Not a trace is left of the great Franciscan cathedral that Bishop Andrew built with the Emperor's funding, or of the other Catholic churches and monasteries, or of the Nestorian churches. All that remains today are a few dozen tombstones (which survived thanks to the efforts of local historian, Wu Linliang). But we also have Bishop Andrew's letter home!

3rd Bishop of Zaytun   Andrew of Perugia, 3rd Bishop of Zaytun presided over one of Zaytun's Franciscan convents (while Peter of Florence supervised the other). Andrew also supervised construction of the east gate Catholic Cathedral, which the emperor not only allowed but actually financed! Following are excerpts from Andrew's fascinating letter home (written in 1326) in which he shed much light on the size of the foreign community, the vast wealth of his Chinese hosts, and the openness of Chinese to foreign trade, philosophy and religion.

Bishop Andrew's Letter Home

"Friar Andrew of Perugia, of the Order of Minor Friars, by Divine permission to the Bishop, to the revered father the Friar Warden of the Convent of Perugia, health and peace in the Lord for ever!

"...through much fatigue and sickness and want, through sundry grievous sufferings and perils by land and sea, plundered even of our habits and tunics, we got at last by God's grace to the city of Camballech, which is the seat of the Emperor the Great Chan, in the year of our Lord's incarnation 1308, as well as I can reckon.

**Headstone of Andrew
3rd Bishop of Zayton**
(Quanzhou Maritime Museum)

"There, after the Archbishop was consecrated...we obtained an Alafa from the emperor for our food and clothing. An Alafa is an allowance for expenses which the emperor grants to the envoys of princes, to orators, warriors, different kinds of artists, jongleurs, paupers, and all sorts of people of all sorts of conditions. And the sum total of these allowances surpasses the revenue and expenditure of several of the kings of the Latin countries.

"As to the wealth, splendor, and glory of this great emperor, the vastness of his dominion, the multitudes of people subject to him, the number and greatness of his cities, and the constitution of the empire, within which no man dares to draw a sword against his neighbor, I will say nothing, because it would be a long matter to write, and would seem incredible to those who heard it. Even I who am here in the country do hear things averred of it that I can scarcely believe...

"There is a great city on the shores of the Ocean Sea, which is called in the Persian tongue Zaytun; and in this city a rich Armenian lady did build a large and fine enough church, which was erected into a cathedral by the Archbishop himself of his own free-will. The lady assigned it, with a competent endowment which she provided during her life and secured by her will at her death, to Friar Gerard the Bishop, and the friars who were with him, and he became accordingly the first occupant of the cathedral."

The cathedral was taken over by Friar and Bishop Peregrine, who died July 7th, 1322, and was succeeded by Andrew, who continues:

"I caused a convenient and handsome church to be built in a certain grove, quarter of a mile outside the city, with all the offices sufficient for twenty-two friars, and with four apartments such that any one of them is good enough for a church dignitary of any rank. In this place I continue to dwell, living upon the imperial dole before-mentioned... Of this allowance I have spent the greatest part in the construction of the church; and I know none among all the convents of our province to be compared to it in elegance and all other amenities...

"'Tis a fact that in this vast empire there are people of every nation under heaven, and every sect, and all and sundry are allowed to live freely according to their creed. For they hold this opinion, or rather this erroneous view, that everyone can find salvation in their own religion. Howbeit we are at liberty to preach without let or hindrance. Of the Jews and Saracens there are indeed no converts, but many of the idolators are baptized; though in sooth many of the baptized walk not rightly in the path of Christianity....

"Farewell in the Lord, father, now and ever. Dated at Zaytun, A.D. 1326, in the month of January."

For Whom the Bells Toll   Of course, the many religions occasionally had their squabbles. One of the most amusing weapons that the Catholics wielded against Muslims was bells!

For some reason, Muslims abhorred bells. Even intrepid Arab traveler Ibn Battuta, who seemingly feared nothing, recounted his "terror and dismay" at the clangor of bells in Caffa. So of course our Saintly Marignolli[3] delighted in letting the Saracens know for whom the bells tolled. In his *Recollections of Travel in the East* he wrote,

"There is Zaytun also, a wondrous fine seaport and a city of incredible size, where our Minors Friars have three very fine churches, passing rich and elegant; and they have a bath also... They have also some fine bells of the best quality, two of which were made to my order, and set up with all due form in the very middle of the Saracen community."

Maybe bells were the Catholics' way of calling Muslims on the prayer carpet for waking them at dawn with the Muslim call to prayer?

The Catholics', Nestorians' and Muslims' keen interest in Chinese souls is not surprising, given that ancient Western tradition claims Chinese are descendents of Noah's son Shem, ancestor of Abraham, patriarch of Islam, Judaism, and Christianity. John Marignolli wrote,

John Marignolli

"Shem was anxious to maintain the worship of the true God, and his history we shall now follow. In the second year after the flood he begat Arfaxat, who ... at the age of thirty-five begat Sela or Sale, by whom India was peopled and divided into three kingdoms. The first of these is called Manzi, the greatest and noblest province in the world, having no paragon in beauty, pleasantness, and extent. In it is that noble city of Campsay, besides Zaytun, Cynkalan [Canton], Janci, and many other cities."

Notes

---

[1] Williams, in Chinese Repository, VI. 149, quote in The Travels of Marco Polo, V. II. P.252

[2] Friar Odoric: arrived in Canton in 1322 with Friar James (Ireland) and traveled on foot to Zaytun. Legend has it that he brought the bones of four missionaries martyred in India to Zaytun, where he buried them. During the voyage, he stilled a storm by tossing one of the bones into the sea. (Evidently the martyr didn't complain of such ill treatment; if he had, he would not have had a leg to stand on). He landed in Canton and traveled overland on foot to Zaytun.

[3] John Marignolli: Giovanni di Marignolli , Franciscan missionary in China from 1342 to 1346 . Born in Florence, Italy, 1290, became a Franciscan and held the chair of theology in the University of Bologna.   Because of a Chinese embassy that arrived in Avignon in 1338, Pope Benedict XII sent Marignolli and other Franciscans to China. At the end of 1341, he crossed the Gobi Desert and was received with honors in the court at Peking. After 3 years in Peking, he traveled through Southern China, and Southeast Asian countries, and arrived back in Italy 15 years after his departure. Years later he wrote of his eastern travels in his "Chronicon Bohemiae."

Chapter 3

Downtown Zaytun Sites

Ashab Mosque (清
静寺) is the perfect
place to begin a down-
town tour because it's a
convenient walk from
the Mosque to half a
dozen other key sites.
Ashab is not only one
of China's ten most
famous temples but also,
I'm told, one of Islam's
top ten holy places.

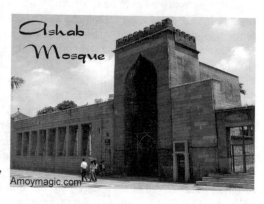

Zaytun once had at least 7 mosques, like the Qingjing Mosque at the southern gate (built by a Muslim from Shiraf, on the Persian Gulf), but Ashab is the only Mosque still standing.

The 2500 square meter Ashab Mosque (also called "Kylin," for Chinese unicorn, or Shenyou Mosque), was built in 1009 A.D., (year 400 of the Muslim calendar). The beautiful imitation of a Damascus mosque was built of blue and white granite, and has a Fengtian altar, Mingshan Chamber, and Prayer Hall. The mosque was renovated in 1310 (Yuan Dynasty) by Ihamed B. Muhammed Gudeish, from Iran.

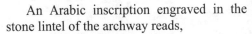

The dome above Fengtian Altar collapsed during a 1607 earthquake, but the magnificent 20m. high vaulted entrance and four walls remain.

Ashab Mosque's portal has four large pointed arches that create three compartments. The second compartment has 99 small pointed arches, which symbolize Allah's 99 appellations of excellence. Above the portal is a square tower with battlements (great spot for taking photos if you can get them to unlock it for you).

An Arabic inscription engraved in the stone lintel of the archway reads,

> "God is witness that there is no God but He, and the angels and all those possessing knowledge stand up for justice. There is no God but He, the mighty, the wise. Verily, in God's sight the true religion is Islam."

To the west of the portal is the former 600 sq. m. worship hall, once covered by a large Islamic dome. A 15th century Chinese record describes the worship hall:

"The halls on the west stand in rows supremely. Their design is different from that of other earthly monasteries, yet swelling and floating, as if emulating a heavenly pavilion."

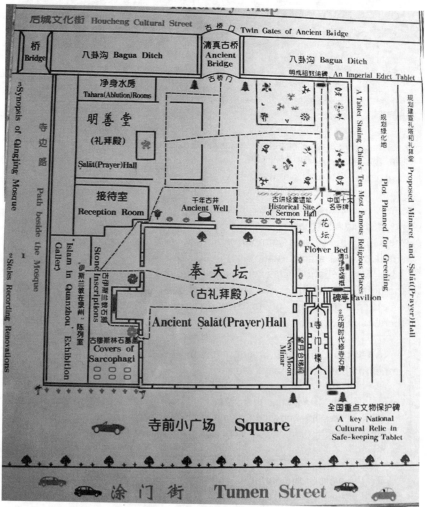

Ashab's Layout

A minaret once towered between the portal and worship hall but it collapsed, and was replaced with a wooden tower. And then a typhoon blew the tower down in 1687—eighty years after an earthquake knocked down the dome.   In the northwest corner of the Mosque are the Ming-shan Hall, Ablution Pavilion and Sermon Hall.

Ashab's 1,000-year-old well

Well Kept The 1,000-year-old-well is said to never run dry, and to always have clean, pure water. A plant grew in its dark depths, but I'm sure it was a clean, pure plant.

Ashab's lotus incense burner

A Buddhist nun demanded to know why Ashab Mosque had a stone incense burner, since Muslims don't use incense. Worse yet, the burner has a lotus leaf motif, suggesting Buddhist influence—and I found the same type of lotus incense burner in Fuzhou's mosque as well. When I suggested the lotus suggested Buddhist influence, an incensed Muslim said, "Buddhists have no monopoly on lotus leaves! All religions use them." But another Muslim confided that the incense burners were adopted because Chinese converts felt Islam wasn't a bona fide religion without incense. (And, of course, Muslims also had strong vested interests in the incense trade!).

1407 Imperial Decree Protecting Islam

Two steles in the Mosque's eastern grounds record the Yuan Dynasty and Ming Dynasty renovations, and the north wall has a 1407 imperial edict protecting Islam.

During the state-funded reconstruction of Ashab Mosque in 1983, workers found several tombs, including that of the son of the Persian prime minister who father was killed in 1312. Other tombstones belonged to Muslims from Tabriz, a Khan (elite muslim) from Khorazm, and a woman from Nabrus in the Eastern Mediterranean.

Restoration   Today, Quanzhou Muslims are not only restoring the place but also building a new Mosque. In addition, the city is building a large Islamic Cultural Heritage Center (under construction now, it dwarfs the adjoining Maritime Museum to the west).

Quanzhou Islamic Cultural Center

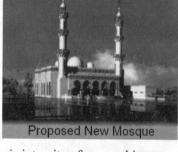
Proposed New Mosque

Quanzhou's comprehensive de-velopment plan insures cultural and historic integrity of new architecture by requiring new construction in "Muslim" areas to retain at least a stylized Islamic flavor. The shopping area across the street from Ashab has an Islamic gate, and even the signboard behind the Mosque has a Middle Eastern flavor!

Islamic Bulletin Board?!

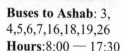
New "Islamic" architecture across the street from ancient Ashab Mosque

Buses to Ashab: 3, 4,5,6,7,16,18,19,26
Hours:8:00 — 17:30   **Phone**: 219-3553

Guandi Temple

(关帝庙)   The ancient temple just east of Ashab Mosque is dedicated to heroic generals Guan Yu and Yue Fei (sort of a "general" purpose temple). Guandi Temple seems to sprawl forever, incense smoke wafting

A "General" Purpose Temple

through the dark recesses hosting a myriad of idols for 24 other famous generals, as well as enlisted heroes for those who have more "private" needs. Cultural relics include Zhu Xi's inscription "Righteousness" , and Zhang Ruitus "Heaven and Earth Imbue the Valiant Spirit." (For a contemporary insight on how such worship begins, visit Hui'ans "PLA Temple" in the walled city of Chongwu).

Getting There: Buses #3,4,5,6,7,8,9,16,18,19, and 26.

Hours: 6:00 — 19:00   **Phone**: 228-6613

Houcheng Tourist Culture Street

(泉州后城旅游文化街)   Quan-zhou's official tourist shopping area, Houcheng Street intersects Tumen Street just east of the mosque and temple, and offers a variety of tourist services and products.   Between Ashab Mosque and the temple is a winding Tourist Shopping Center

Mao Memorabilia Shop

with vendors offering everything from replica antique coins and copper bowls to jade jewelry, gramophones, and 60s era Chairman Mao alarm clocks and watches (which are increasingly popular, so don't expect to land a real Mao clock for only a few mao).   After emptying your pockets, walk west a block to the Confucian Hall

Confucian Literary Temple

Imperial Examination Cells (Smith, 1908)

"Failure to obtain a coveted prize never baffles or discourages the indefatigable competitor. In some cases the contest continues a lifetime with the prize never won. For example at a single prefecture 10,000 candidates presented themselves, under the old regime, at the regular examination. Among them were found the grandfathers, sons, and grandsons, all competing for the same prize, i.e., the same degree. In 1889 the Governor General of Fukien reported that at the autumnal examination in Foochow there were nine candidates over eighty, and one over ninety years old. At still another, thirty five competitors were over eighty and eighteen over ninety. Such indomitable perseverance along educational lines...has been seldom witnessed outside of China. If ever her educational methods conform to Western ideas...Chinese scholarship is destined to take first rank."

Rev. Pitcher (In and about Amoy, 1912, p.84)

Quanzhou Confucian Literary Temple, a block West of Ashab Mosque, on the north side of Tumen Street, showcases Quanzhou's educational legacy, with life-size wax sculptures of Quanzhou's literati.

Confucian Literary Temple

Called "Seashore Zhoulu" (something like "Academy/Scholar Upon the Sea") Quanzhou has been a wellspring of literary talent and leadership. From the Tang to the Qing Dynasty (about 1,100 years), the city produced 2,473 successful candidates in the highest imperial examinations, and 950 famous scholars produced 2,083 influential works. In addition, twenty prime ministers came from Quanzhou.

Confucian Temple

Famous Quanzhou intellectuals have included writers Ou'yang Zhan, Wang Shenzhong and Huang Kehui, historians Xiaqing, Liang Kejia, Huang Fengxiang and He Qiaoyuan, and philosophers Li Zhi, Cai Qing, Chen Chen and Cai Ding. Quanzhou military talents have included Ding Gongchen, Zeng Gongliang, Yu Daqin, Zheng Chengyong, Su Song, Li Guangdi, etc.

Confucius would have been proud!
Getting There: Buses #1, 3, 18
Hours: 8:00 — 17:30   **Phone**: 228-3914

Anxi also has a famous Confucius Temple (安溪文庙), built in 1001 A.D. Or is it a Confusion Temple…?

Anxi Confusion Temple? A Quanzhou English map has a location for the "Anxi Confusion Temple." I'm not absolutely certain it is a typo.

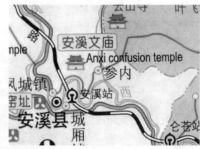

Given that Taoism and Confucianism, two of China's main religions, are 180 degrees apart in philosophy, it is surprising that in some temples, people worship both. Unlike Confucianism, which emphasizes absolute obedience, conformity, standards, and education to preserve them, Taoism is the Montessori approach to enlightenment. Taoism means "The Way" (as New Testament Christianity also meant "The Way"), and is based on the teachings of Lao Tzu in 6th Century B.C. China. But with Taoism, the way is relative for there are no standards for proper behavior or right and wrong. All is relative. The emphasis is individual freedom, loose government, and mystical experience.

Not surprisingly, the powers that be preferred Confucius to Lao Tzu—though not in the sage's own lifetime....

A Brief Bio of Confucius (Adapted from *Amoy Magic*) As a youth, Confucius mastered poetry and history classics, and the six arts (ritual, music, archery, charioteering, calligraphy and arithmetic). In his 30s, he became a teacher and devoted his life to insuring that Chinese for the next 3000 years followed suit.

Confucius

Confucius humbly claimed to be a common man of ordinary intellect, so anyone could follow his lead in seeking perfection through study and conformity to society. But few wanted to follow Confucius' lead because he was usually jobless, homeless, and half-starved.

Confucius' failures ate at him. He said, "It is these things that cause me concern: failure to cultivate virtue, failure to explore in depth what I have learned, inability to do what I know is right, and inability to reform myself when I have defects."

I think what really ate at him was his wife, who was also homeless and half-starved – not choice ingredients in the elixir of marital bliss.

While claiming to be just one of the boys, the unemployed Confucius said he was unstoppable and immortal until his heavenly mandate was completed. "If Heaven does not intend this culture to be destroyed, then what can the men of K'uang do to me?"

Not much, except keep him unemployed. So at age 56 he left the inhospitable leaders of Lu, who still weren't hiring, and spent 12 years traveling about with a slowly growing following. He returned home at age 67 and died 6 years later, leaving behind 3,000 disciples who were usually jobless, homeless and half-starved. But they kept alive the teachings that would become dear to 2400 years of imperial hearts.

Confucians taught a grassroots philosophy that the foundation of society is filial piety. Obedience to father and elders and magistrates and emperor guarantees social order, stability, and peace. Deviations, of any kind (like preferring coffee over tea) insure anarchy.

Emperors loved Confucius's emphasis on obedience, but his warning that unjust governments would be overthrown did not go over as well. In 231 B.C., the emperor tried to eliminate Confucius' influence by destroying every book in China, but someone missed a few volumes. Confucians crawled back out of the woodwork, regained the upper hand, and have been stacking China's deck ever since (while being careful to remove all the wild cards).

My Favorite Confucian Quotes

Fishy Fishing, 7.27 子钓而不纲. "Confucius fished but didn't use a net." (No wonder he was poor)

On Women: 17:25, 子曰：唯女子与小人为难养也，近之则不恭，远之则怨 "Girls are the most impossible; too close and they lose their humility; keep your distance and they're disgruntled." (Lesson: You can't win!)

志于道，据于德，依于仁，游于艺 "Aspire to the principle, behave with virtue, abide by benevolence, and immerse yourself in the arts."

"Wherever you go, go with all your heart." **Amen.**

Quanzhou Puppets!

Puppet Museum Sign

"Quanzhou puppet art has a long history and has been inherited for generations. It is well known at home and abroad as a bright pearl in the treasure house of Quanzhou. On display are master puppet pieces, rich contented articles and photographs, which vividly present the exquisite carved puppet heads and the unique craftsmanship of the puppetmaking, and also shows you the puppeteer's high skill of the string and glove puppet manipulation, as well as the Quanzhou puppet arts' influence in Taiwan and abroad. All of these will present to you a splendid picture of this art. Please step into the gallery of Quanzhou puppet art. Enjoy its magic."

Puppets! Quanzhou is the home of China's marionettes, with more puppets than parliament! Later in this chapter we will visit the absolutely delightful Puppet Troup Museum, but while we're in the area, let's stop in at the Chen

Puppet Museum (behind Ashab Mosque)

family's topnotch puppet museum right behind the Ashab Mosque.

This fine museum has a broad display not only of Quanzhou's famous marionettes but also of Jinjiang hand puppets and many other forms of puppetry. Nicely laid out displays show how the wooden creatures are crafted lovingly from blocks of camphor wood until, in the hands of a master, they spring to life with more gusto than Pinocchio on the trail of the Blue Fairy.

Camphor wood comes to life!

After the museum, walk north (towards the mountains) past the Overseas Chinese hotel, and at Fengze St. (丰泽街—the Copper Buddha Temple and lake will be on your right), turn left. About 100 meters past the KFC is the puppet shop, with a broad assortment of puppets, Chinese souvenirs, full-sized Chinese costumes, and a broad array of silk cloth. In the alley behind are other shops with classical Chinese musical instruments.

Puppet Shop

Embroidering puppet costumes

Mr. David Zeng (曾国恒), who works with Quanzhou TV when he's not pulling other strings, can arrange for you to watch artisans carving camphor puppet heads or creating beautifully embroidered puppet costumes. And for the merriest marionette treat, turn to the end of this chapter for the Quanzhou Marionette Puppet Troupe Museum!(page 72)

Historic Zhongshan Rd (中山路)   From the Puppet Shop, head west , and turn north on the ancient Zhongshan Rd, with its endless shops and the leafy canopy of trees that make a stroll pleasant on the sultriest days. Notice the Islamic architecture.

Zhongshan Rd.

Muslim Chinese Life in U.S.!

I particularly like the building with Islamic windows above and a "Fun" clothing store with "Life in U.S." motto below. The city is becoming almost as cosmopolitan as ancient Zaytun.

Hidden Treasures   Head off down just about any of the narrow side streets and you'll come to hidden treasures like the home of the Qing Dynasty Minister of Defense, Huang Zonghan (黄宗汉,1803-1864 A.D.） who succeeded the famous Opium era Commissioner, Lin Zexu.

Home of Huang Zonghan (黄宗汉) (On Zhenfu Lane, 镇抚巷).   According to Qu Weiwei, a tourism student at Overseas Chinese Univ. who acted as my guide a few days, Huang Zonghan was born in Quanzhou, and was governor of Guangdong and Guangxi

Huang Zonghan's Home

provinces (两广总督) from 1856-1861. Huang fought so bravely against the Taiping rebels that Emperor Xianfeng (咸丰) personally inscribed a stele with 忠勤正直—"Loyal, Diligent, Honest". It was a great honor. Unfortunately, the Emperor stole the stele back when his hero became embroiled in a political scandal, and the stele is probably gravel by now.

Huang Zonghan's House (and bicycle)

Overseas Chinese University Professor Cheng Lichu (程立初), Huang Zonghan's descendant, gave us a tour. He pointed out the granite stele engraved, right to left, with Da Si Ma (大司马) and said, "Written by the Emperor himself! Only the Emperors could write that well."

Written by the Emperor himself!

1 Million Yuan Restoration! Professor Cheng said the restoration, which received no government funding, cost his family one million Yuan. I could not imagine how they

1 Million Yuan on Restoration!

could pour that much money in fixing up such an old house until he showed me the intricately carved woodwork, and the granite columns in the courtyard. "The originals were wood," he said, "But trees don't come that big nowadays."

Professor Cheng claimed he could easily earn the million Yuan back if he needed it. (If he doesn't need it, Quanzhou Overseas Chinese

University must pay a lot more than we get at Xiamen University!). Professor Cheng claimed that he was offered 10,000 Yuan for just one potted tree—and refused. Maybe he's saving it for when he's really up a tree?

Professor Cheng and 10,000 Yuan Tree

A Xu Beihong Original?

Prof. Cheng also said he could get one million Yuan just by selling the painting of a matriarch that hangs above the family ancestral shelf. It didn't look that hot to me, but I can't tell a black velvet Elvis from a Van Gogh. According to the professor, this dour dowager was painted by none other than renowned Chinese artist Xu Beihong (徐悲鸿)!

Xu Beihong (1895—1953), most famous for his horse paintings, studied in France and adapted his techniques to Chinese painting. He survived his early years in part by painting portraits of wealthy clients, so Huang Zonghan's painting may indeed be a genuine Xu Beihong piece.

View samples of Xu's innovative art at:
http://www.eastart.net/articles/xubei hong/index_ytjjxbh.htm

Many Mansions   As Professor Cheng showed us some more of Huang Zonghan's 14 mansions (lots of wives, probably), we came upon several ladies having tea in a tight lane between two beautiful brick buildings. A great photo op, you can enter that picturesque lane at #22 Jade Rhinoceros Lane(Yuxi Lane, 玉犀巷,which is north of and parallel to Furen Xiang). We exited the north end, and then entered the next doorway on the left to find a delightful courtyard that was refreshingly cool, in spite of the oppressive heat. "Beats air conditioning!" the Professor said.

"The straight and narrow"

Taihu Stone

Tie Who?   A man was scooping leaves from a spring fed carp pond with a net on a long bamboo pole. The carp looked old enough (and complacent enough) to have lived there since the days of Huang Zonghen himself.

Towards the back of the courtyard was a massive jumble of outlandish stones. Professor Cheng said, "Taihu Stone!"

"Tie who?" I said. (Maybe a relative of Sharon Stone?).

"That's right!" he said. "Jiangsu Province Tai Lake (太湖) stones, are prized by miniature landscape artists throughout China. These are sold by the pound now. Imagine what this is worth!" Given what he's asking for his paintings and trees, I didn't want to ask.

Taihu Stone Story

By Miss Qu Weiwei (曲微微)

Tie who?

Taihu Lake's Taihu Stone, also called Dongting Stone, comes in two kinds: that from water and that from land. Water stones are of course better because the water has carved it into more elegant shapes. While Taihu Stone is usually white, black and green stones have also been found.

Taihu stones became popular in the Tang Dynasty, and from the Song Dynasty have been widely used in rich people's gardens. Even the emperor asked that Taihu stones be shipped to his palace.

The famous novel Shui Hu Zhuan (Outlaws of the Marsh) mentions Taihu stones in some chapters. Today, the most valuable Taihu Stone is in Shanghai's Yu Garden. It is named Yu Linglong (exquisite jade, 玉玲珑).

Chinese think Taihu Stones are beautiful precisely because they are so crinkled, thin, holey--downright ugly. This reflects the Taoist philosophy in which when something reaches the peak it crosses over. So Taihu stones are so ugly they are beautiful.

[I guess there is hope for Bill Brown yet!]

National Treasure   The professor pointed out a glistening cave stone and exclaimed, "This is a priceless National Level Treasure! Look closely and you can see that the natural design resembles snow on winter plums—like a Chinese abstract painting."

I guess I'll never paint Chinese abstracts, because I saw neither snow nor plums, but I did appreciate the stones natural beauty (I've collected minerals and stones since I was six, and our apartment is crammed with a few hundred pounds of specimens). But it didn't appear that local residents were so enamored of the stone. They were using it as a mop rack. When I aimed my camera, Miss Qu Weiwei started to remove the mops, but the professor said, "Leave them there so people can see how we care for such treasures!"

National Treasure

Getting to Huang Zonghan's Home: it's but a 5 minute walk from the Copper Buddha Temple (Tongfo Si, 铜佛寺),on Furen Lane (Furen Xiang, 敷仁巷), between Zhongshan Rd. and Nanjun Xiang (南俊巷) —just north of Fengze St. (丰泽街).

Zhongshan Shopping Quanzhou is a shopper's paradise, with wall-to-wall shops—and name brands at that!   Stores that don't hawk name brands make up for it with grandiloquent names—like the sports shop called "Standard Physical Culture Stores."

Good sports

I can't get into shopping like Susan Marie. Sue can happily spend half a day sifting through a display of cotton slippers or tea towels, whereas I can make it through the Mall of America in minutes—with wallet intact.   But I do enjoy meeting the people in Chinese shops. They're friendly, and invariably invite you in for tea before getting down to business. And bargaining can be a real eye-opener…

One Size Fits All!
(Adapted from *Amoy Magic*)

My wife Susan Marie rummaged through a pile of sweaters in a Longyan City street stall. She finally found one she liked, but it was too small. "Bu yao jin!" [不要紧! No problem!] the lady said. "It stretches when you wear it!"

"I don't know," Sue said.   She

"Shrinks when washed!"

eventually found another sweater she liked, but it was far too large.

"Bu yao jin!" the same lady said. "It shrinks when you wash it!"

Fortunately, even the die-hard "one size fits all" types are good natured about it, and will laugh as they hit you with, "I'm losing money, but hey! We're friends!" (Though you met only ten minutes earlier). Or they toss out a line common in many countries, "I'll sell to you at a loss because it is bad luck if the 1st customer of the day doesn't buy something" (and this at 3

Quanzhou girls got style!

p.m.). The one that really gets to me is, "Chinese New Year is coming up so I'm selling everything at a loss or I won't make enough to return home to my family."

But how do I know when it's a "line" and when it's true? Besides, 1

Happy Shoppers

Yuan means much more to them than to me, so I dicker, but only out of obligation, on pure principle. And several times, kind shopkeepers have laughed and sold their wares for less than I asked—or given me something in addition for free!

So yes, bargaining *can* be fun. Even my little friend Emma got caught up in bargaining for a bear, and just bearly got them down to her budget (and that's the bear truth).

Emma's 1st Bargain!
(she bearly got it)

Quannan Protestant Church (Zhongshan Rd) Zaytun's Nestorian Christianity and Franciscan Catholic cathedrals and monasteries vanished, and while Islam did keep a toehold, many Hui's sole claim to orthodoxy is their refusal to eat pork. But churches have reentered the scene over the past 140 years, and Quanzhou now has Catholic churches and over 170 Protestant Churches!

Over 170 Quanzhou Churches

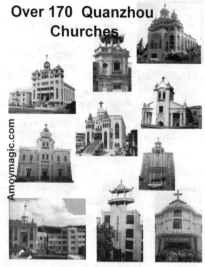

Amoymagic.com

Pastor Su Weiyuan 苏伟垣

Pastor Su Weiyuan 苏伟垣, of the South Street Church (泉南堂, on historic Zhongshan Rd., south of historic Pizza Hut) kindly gave me an outline of the history of Protestantism in Quanzhou, and also allowed me to use information and photos from "Unforgettable Journey—Fifty Years for Fujian Christian Churches on the Three-Self,"[1] for which Pastor Su was Editor-in-Chief.

The first Opium War opened five treaty ports, including Amoy and Fuzhou, but Quanzhou remained off limits to foreigners. So in 1856, Rev. Carstairs Douglas, a Scottish minister in the English Presbyterian Mission who had arrived in Amoy in July, 1955, sailed in secret (Stealth Junk?) to southern Quanzhou's Anhai Town. In 1863, he moved on to Quanzhou, and in 1866,

they opened the first Protestant church right across from Kaiyuan Temple, where they preached right in the temple gates. Infuriated scholars burned the church down, whereupon the Christians took a gamble on a gambling den's location a few blocks away on Zhongshan Rd.

General Shilang, the Chinese hero we'll encounter in the Nan'an chapter, had a house and rockery garden on the church's new site, but it had fallen to ruins and become a gambling den. The Christians bought Shilang's land and set up shop again, and once again the scholars burned the church down. And here is where being a foreigner during the Opium Era came in handy. Complaints were registered with the British forces in nearby Amoy, and in 1876, the compensation extracted from the perpetrators was used to help build a new church of brick and timber, as well as a parsonage for the foreign pastor (the first Chinese pastor was Chen Xuanling (陈宣令), from Zhangzhou, in 1886.

Quannan Church was renovated in the 1890s, and rebuilt in 1927, but by the 90s it had deteriorated so badly that it was razed to the ground in 2002. A new church seating 3,000 will be finished by the end of 2,003.

New Quannan Church
(opens end of 2003)

Minnan Dialect and Missions   Our vertical province has more dialects than any place else in China. In some places, villagers cannot understand neighbors only 3 km away! Yet ironically, instead of hindering Christian work this actually worked out to their advantage. Before missionaries could get into China, they worked in other Southeast Asian countries, most of which had large populations of overseas Chinese. Most overseas Chinese, of course, were from southern Fujian, and so the missionaries learned Minnan dialect. Once China opened up, foreign missionaries converged upon southern Fujian because they already knew the language. Faced with widespread illiteracy, they developed romanization schemes and Minnan language dictionaries and references. Rev. Carstairs Douglas' *Dictionary of the Vernacular or Spoken Language of Amoy*, published in 1873, remains a standard reference work even today. Unfortunately, he died only 4 years later of cholera at the age of 46 (having spent 22 of his years in China).[2] But these early foreigners' legacy in education continues at places like Peiyuan High School…

Peiyuan High School

(培元中学) Just West of Kaiyuan Temple (we're headed there soon!), Peiyuan was started in 1904 by Mr. Anderson (安礼逊牧师), of the London Presbyterian Mission, and received the patronage of none other than Dr. Sun Yat-sen!

Peiyuan High School -- 100 Years of Excellence

Rev. Anderson
London Presbyterian Mission

Rev. Anderson's father was one of the men who had helped free Dr. Sun when he was kidnapped by the Qing in London. To express his appreciation, Dr. Sun encouraged Chinese to contribute towards building Anderson's school, and in 1920 he wrote an inscription for the school. In 1980, his wife, Soong Ching Ling (Honorary President of China) wrote another inscription to the left of her husband's.

Dr. Sun's inscription reads, right to left, 共进大同 (Gong Jin Da Tong): "All Enter Future Heaven." Madame Soong's inscription, read left to right, is 为国树人 (Wei Guo Shu Ren): "Bring Up People for the Country."

Peiyuan Headmaster and Dr. Bill

Anderson Library, built in 1927, was Quanzhou's tallest building (aside from the East and West Pagodas)! It resembles a church inside, perhaps because until the 1950s it was also used for church services.

The Philippine extension was established in the 1920s, and Taiwan's 1st of 3 branches was begun in the 1950s. The school's recent expansion and renovation has been possible in part because of generous gifts from alumni and overseas Chinese, and the school has recently bought a factory site to the south for campus expansion.

Anderson Library
(Quanzhou's tallest bldg. in 1927!)

Vice Premier Li Lanqing (李岚清) visited Peiyuan in 1994 and wrote the large inscription that is now beside the 300 year old tree.

Peiyuan High School

Vice Premier Li Lanqing's Inscription

New building under construction

In 2004, the school celebrates 100 years of producing graduates who have gone on to distinctive careers in business, academics and government, and the school has branches overseas.   Many of them exemplify the school motto found on the wall beside Li Langqing's inscription:

Truth   **Freedom**   **Service**

Community Service   Peiyuan's motto seems to have also been adopted by Quanzhou Christians. Since Fujian's church services were begun again in 1979, the province has opened over 1500 churches, including over 170 churches in Quanzhou alone—and community service is a big part of Quanzhou Christians' lives. In 1998, Fujian churches donated over 800,000 RMB and over 100,000 articles of clothing to flood victims along the Yangzi, Songhua and Nan Rivers. The Quanzhou church donated 10,000 Yuan to Anxi's Bailai County for renovating primary school classrooms, and giving free medical care to Yongchun minorities. Contributions to medicine and education are also being made by individual Christians like cardiologist Dr. Lin Yinwang (林应望)

Dr. Lin Yinwang

Dr. Lin is former director of Internal Medicine in Quanzhou's #1 Hospital, as well as Vice Director of the 10th Standing Committee of the

Quanzhou Municipal People's Congress and representative of the 6th, 7th, and 8th PPC   Dr. Lin established a cardiovascular clinic in Jinjiang #1 Hospital, and has published dozens of papers in medical journals. Other Christian doctors also volunteer their services in clinics around the city.

Volunteer Medical Work

Dr. Sun Yat-sen & the Dentist
This Zhongshan Rd. dental clinic
(鲤中卫生院，二楼), just south of
the clock tower by the ancient Pizza
Hut, proves that in ancient Zaytun,
virtually every corner has something of interest if you know what to
look for.

The modern second floor clinic
of Dr. Sheng Mingjie (盛明捷) has
an inscription by Dr. Sun Yat-sen
on the wall! It was written for his

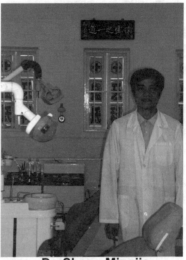

Dr. Sheng Mingjie
(Sun Yat-sen inscription in back)

Dr. Sun Yat-sen's Inscription

grandfather, Sheng Jiuchang (盛九
昌). Elder Mr. Sheng, also a dentist,
was one of Dr. Sun's soldiers-in-arms.
Dr. Sun's inscription reads, right to
left, 卫生之一道. Weisheng Zhi Yi
Dao. I think it roughly means that the
mouth is an important part of sanita-
tion. A copy of the inscription is on
the outside of the building, near the
roof (the original, by the way, is in a
Beijing museum).

Kaiyuan Temple

"...there were three thousand monks and eleven thousand idols...All the dishes which they offer to be eaten are piping hot so that the smoke riseth up in the face of the idols... But all else they keep for themselves and gobble up. And after such fashion as this they reckon that they feed their gods well."

Friar Odoric

East Pagoda

Take a left at the Zhongshan Rd. clock tower and you'll come to Kaiyuan Temple (circa 686 A.D.), one of China's most important temples and, at 78,000 sq.m., Fujian's largest religious center. And that's not all! Kaiyuan's inexpensive ticket gains you entry to half a dozen other famous sites, including a tree that's a bloomin' miracle.

Timely Landmark

Miraculous Mulberry-Lotus Tree

According to legend, Mr. Huang Shougong, owner of a mulberry field, dreamed that a Buddhist monk asked him to donate land for a temple. Mr. Huang threw out a fleece. "I'll donate the land if this mulberry tree blossoms with white lotus flowers."

Three days later, white lotus flowers bloomed on the mulberry tree. Mr. Huang said, "It's a bloomin' miracle!" and ceded the land. (Though given Quanzhou folk's prowess at making silk flowers, I wonder if Mr. Huang thought to make sure the lotus blossoms were real?)

Miraculous Mulberry-Lotus Tree

Barbarian-befuddling Dates, Mus, Li way, & Other Taels

An English brochure claimed Kaiyuan Temple was built in the 2nd year of Chuigong in the Tang Dynasty. This is the Chinese' singularly barbarian-befuddling way of saying "686 A.D." Why they persist in such dating I'm not sure. Even many Chinese can't remember the years of different dynasties, much less the reigns within them.

I don't give a fig for Chinese dates, but weights and measures are worse. For example, Xiamen's Huli Hill cannon cost 60,000 taels (tael= 38 grams) of silver, and Quanzhou's Luoyang Bridge, built in 1059, cost 1.4 million liang of silver. But what did silver cost in the 1800s, or in 1059?

If the MBA Center starts paying me in taels or liangs I'm quitting.

Another pet peeve is the "mu," which is not cow talk but a unit of land measure. The Chinese dictionary said, "100 mu = 1 qing, currently called shimu, 1 shimu = 60 sq. zhang or 666.7 sq. m."

I don't want to have a cow over mus, but sometimes they're enough to make me bleat. As for lengths and distances... An English brochure boasts Anping Bridge is 8,110 chi long and 16 chi wide--but what's a chi? And a Quanzhou sign says, "Shaolin Temple 600 m." but I measured it and it's 1.1 km. Granted, the road winds a lot, and the Kungfu kicking monks probably fly direct, but I'm not the first to go the extra mile when tackling Chinese distances. In 1912, Rev. Philip Pitcher[3] wrote,

"These distances may not be accepted as entirely accurate. They are only approximate. When one comes to calculating distances in this part of China he meets with difficulties at once, chief among them being the difference in the length of the li (lee) [about 1/3 of a mile] in different parts of this district. There are long li and short li; there are mandarin li and the common ordinary country li. The difference between these two is considerable, a mandarin li being one fourth shorter."

Recently, a Chinese friend boasted that Anping Bridge is 5 li long. I wonder if he meant long li, short li, mandarin li or common country li? I guess I'll just have to give him a little li way.

Key Kaiyuan Sites

Kaiyuan's main areas include "Purple Clouds Screen," "Hall of Heavenly Devarajas," "Great Buddhist Hall," "Sweet Dew Altar of Precepts," and "Depository of Buddhist Texts" (With over 37,000 volumes of rare Buddhist scriptures and relics). Other sites

Kaiyuan Temple

include "Sanders Shade Temple," "Mini-Kaiyuan Temple," "Hall of Benifence," "Triumph Temple," "Land and Water Temple," and the five level, octagonal "Ganlujie Altar," where Buddhists underwent rites to become monks and nuns. Ganlujie Altar is the largest and best preserved altar of its kind in China, with the Supreme Buddha Losana sitting on a lotus platform of 1,000 lotus leaves, each having a six centimeter engraved Buddha.

Ring a bell?

Lugang Iron Bell was cast in 1837 and presented to Kaiyuan Temple by 46 companies of Lugang, Taiwan. Supposedly, the bell is so loud it can be heard all the way to Luoyang Bridge on the coast.

The Buddhist Scripture Library boasts over 37,000 volumes of rare Buddhist scriptures and relics. Two carved stone poles bear carvings of Shiva the Destroyer, a member of the Hindu trinity (which includes Brahma and Vishnu). The poles were transported to Quanzhou from a collapsed Indian temple. But no one seems to mind the mixed motifs. In fact, Chinese temples often have Buddhist, Confucian and Taoist idols and rites in the same temple, as if the more the merrier (or perhaps they are just covering all of their bases).

Purple Haze and Buddhist Angels

Purple clouds surrounded Kaiyuan's 1,387 sq. m. main hall while under construction, so it was dubbed Purple Cloud Hall (which inspired Jimi Hendrix' "Purple Haze?").   The great hall had 100 granite pillars, so it was also called 100-Pillar-Hall.   But the hall's most unique feature is its 24 flying bat-winged angels (apsaras)--one for each division of the traditional Chinese solar year.

Bats symbolize evil and death for Westerners, but Chinese think they are lucky because "bat" (fu, 蚨) and "fortune" (fu,福) are homonyms. The batty angels (or "wonderful music birds") protrude from pillar brackets and help support the uniquely complicated beam structure. Their outstretched arms bear fruit, scholars' "four treasures" (writing brush, ink slab, ink stick and paper), and traditional Chinese musical instruments.

Amoymagic.com

I thought horns were forbidden within city limits?

(Across from Quanzhou Bus Station)

Kaiyuan's angels can't be photographed without written permission from the provincial Religious Affairs Bureau, so I applied and waited to see what would develop. I just got negatives. But Quanzhou does have other angels—at the musical fountain across from the Quanzhou long distance bus station.

Hindu Influence The Hindu relics scattered throughout the Kaiyuan temple are reminders of Zaytun's extensive early contacts with India—largely with Tamil merchants. The unusual Indian sphinx in the temple's base was

added early on, but the columns with Indian carvings behind Kaiyuan's main hall were scavenged from an Indian temple about four centuries ago when the father of Koxinga (Nan'an chapter) helped rebuild the temple. The Twin Pagodas also show Indian influence, in part because an Indian monk supervised one of the renovations.

East and West Pagodas The East and West Pagodas flanking Kaiyuan Temple are the best preserved stone pagodas in China. They were first built of wood and stone, then brick, and later stone. Modeled after the great wooden pavilions of the Central Plains, they have withstood 1,000 years of earthquakes and tourists, thanks to their Song Dynasty reconstruction, which took 22 years.

The East Pagoda (Zhen-guo—"nation-protecting"), a brochure says, was built of wood in 670 A.D. (I thought of writing "1st Year of Qianfeng in the Tang Dynastyo"—just to see if my Chinese readers could figure it out!). It was later rebuilt as a 48.24 m stone pagoda.

The West Pagoda (Renshou —"merit and longevity") was built in 916. Both of the five story octagonal structures are carved top to bottom with vivid relief sculptures, and warriors are carved into the niches of each story. Legend has it that

Twin Pagodas of Old Quanzhou

when the East Pagoda had been built up to the fourth level, abbot Faquan died, and the remaining construction was supervised by Tianxi, a monk from India who had come to Quanzhou to preach Buddhist scriptures. This resulted in an unusual marriage of Chinese and Indian motifs, and a bit of monkey business as well.

Bearded Bodhisattva

Bearded Beauty   The West Pagoda has two highly unusual carvings. One is of the Monkey King, and the other is of a moustached Goddess of Mercy. Guanyin was originally a man, but Chinese woman needed a female to pray to (and male gods were not seen as compassionate or merciful; just look at their expressions!). California has so many religions, one wonders why this Deity in Drag hasn't caught on?

Monkey   Business
Some folks go ape over the West Pagoda's Monkey King carvings, claiming they are the origin of the Monkey King story since the carvings predate, by hundreds of year, the 16th century epic "Journey to the West," which popularized the simian saint. In all likelihood, this monkey business began with the monkey-god Hanuman in the Indian epic, Ramayana. After all, an Indian monk took charge of the pagodas' renovations.

Monkey King

Song Dynasty Ship

To the right of Kaiyuan, past the Buddhist museum, is the display for the Song Dynasty (960-1279) ship unearthed in Houzhu Harbor in 1974. . The 24.2 m by 9.15 m. ship had 13 separate watertight compartments made the ship

Incensed Trader's Unsinkable Ship

virtually unsinkable—at least until it sunk. A typhoon snapped off the mast and the ship went down 100 meters offshore, fully laden with Southeast Asian products, as well as 2350 kg of incense wood—which no doubt incensed the Muslim owners to no end.

Unsinkable segmented hull "Oh, Jack!"

Watertight compartments were not adopted by Western shipbuilders until the 19th century, and in the early 20th century this amazingly innovative technique was used on the unsinkable Titanic, which promptly sunk. "Oh, Jack!"

For more about the Muslim incense trade, and to actually meet a descendant of the incensed Muslim's who owned the unsinkable Song Dynasty sunken ship, turn to the Dehua/Yongchun chapter. (p.214) And now… we'll find out who's really pulling the strings in Quanzhou, the marionette capital of China!

Quanzhou
——Marionette Capital of China!

International Puppet Festivals Quanzhou was selected to host the International Puppet Festivals in 1986, 1990 and 2000 for one good reason: this ancient center of commerce, philosophy and religion is also the home of Chinese marionettes!

Of course, Quanzhou has many unique crafts, including exquisite paper lanterns, bamboo weaving, porcelain, wood sculpture, tree root carving, paper weaving, lacquer ware, clay sculptures, miniature flour carvings, and 1700 years of Hui'an stone carving, but the icing on the cultural cake is puppets, which stand camphor heads and shoulders above the rest.

Mr. Xia Rong Feng

Quanzhou Marionette Troupe (泉州 木偶剧团) has thrilled audiences in over 30 countries and regions, including performances in London's Royal Festival Hall. Over 30 puppeteers manipulate the puppets while singing to the background of a full Chinese orchestra. Unfortunately, it's hard to catch their acts at home, but you can arrange a once-in-a-lifetime command performance for only 2,000 Yuan. Contact the Vice Director of Performers, Mr. Xia Rong Feng (夏荣峰), at 237-5497. Mobile Phone: 13959798518. He can also arrange for a tour of the marvelous Puppet Troupe's museum.

Chinese puppetry dates back at least to the Han Dynasty 2000 years ago, though legend has it the art began 3000 years ago with King Mu of the Zhou Dynasty. While returning from hunting in the Kunlun mountains, he saw a carpenter, Yanshi, giving a song and dance performance with his wooden dolls. The art evolved over the past two to three thousand years, and reached its epitome in Quanzhou, which has the only Chinese puppets that boast their own musical repertoire performed on unique musical instruments, with over 300 songs and tunes written for the 700+ traditional puppet shows.

Puppet Master Composes

These miraculous marionettes have more strings attached than a henpecked husband. When deftly wielded by a master puppeteer, 14 to 36 strings bring the wooden folk to life as they strut and fret with abandon across intricate Chinese stages.

Unlike Western puppeteers, who work mainly with the control, Chinese puppeteers also manipulate groups of strings with their fingers. The longer the strings (up to 2 meters!), the more difficult to operate, but the more expressive the puppets can become as they portray men and women of all ages and professions—or even spirits or wild animals.

Who's pulling whose strings now?
Amoymagic.com

Puppets make love and war, bicker and barter, dance, jog and somersault. Their deft hands even retrieve objects from the stage floor! Maybe their lips move too, because Jimmy sure fell for this fellow (who robs cradles too). But everything hinges on puppeteers like Mr. Xia Rong Feng (夏荣峰), Quanzhou Puppet Troupe's Vice Director of Performers (who kindly gave us a tour and a delightful demonstration).

Puppeteers, who often begin training as children, may take 5 years to learn the basics, and over 20 years to completely master the 30+ strings! The sheer complexity of marionettes is amazing. They have a torso, limbs, strings and a hollow wooden head (usually camphor or willow) with internal mechanisms to move the lips and eyes. They have civilian hands to hold pens and cups or swing fans, and military hands to brandish swords, spears, and other weapons. There are even three types of feet: bare, booted, and womanly.

No wonder modern youth aren't keen on devoting their lives to mastering puppetry, and the camphor creatures are getting more complex by the year.

Robbing the cradle!
Amoymagic.com

Modern Puppetry   During the late Qing Dynasty, puppeteers like Lin Chengchi could make their puppets draw swords and open umbrellas. But today's generation of puppeteers are as good, or better. And for all their skill, they are continuing to perfect their craft to create utterly breathtaking puppets and performances. Modern stages are deeper, allowing the puppets greater freedom of movement, and allowing the use of different types of puppets simultaneously. For example, the Iron-fan Princess in "Flaming Mountain" is manipulated with strings, poles and fingers.

In *Taming the Monkey*, the simian puppet monkeys about doing everything from riding a bicycle to playing a guitar. In *Drunken Zhong Kui*, Kui fails the imperial examination simply because he is so ugly. After he commits suicide, the King of Hell appoints him "Master demon chaser," but he is so overwhelmed by the number of wicked demons and ghosts that he turns to drink. But in the end he goes on the wagon, and then devotes himself to an eternal battle against wickedness. It's a hell of a story.

Carrying the Tradition Abroad   The Quanzhou Puppet Troupe gave a short workshop to 11 British puppeteers and puppet lovers in London's Little Angel Puppet Theater. Christopher Leith had worked with marionettes for over 35 years and still found the training tough. Still, the Chinese said they'd done well in such a short time, and should be up to snuff in a couple

Over 30 countries and regions!

of years (a long time for us Westerners, but nothing for Chinese who spend decades at it).

Crafting Puppet Heads   Crafting quality camphor wood puppet heads is a vanishing art. People just aren't patient enough nowadays to spend 10 to 15 years mastering this exacting craft. Of the few dozen puppet head makers left in Quanzhou, only ten to twenty make quality puppets. The rest churn out mass produced heads (or, worse yet, press out plastic heads, which may look the same but don't have the soul of the genuine wooden folk).

Amoymagic.com

Puppet heads begin life as a block of camphor wood which is cut to a rough form, sanded, then carved with finer detail. After a coat of paint, and then gloss, further details and hair are added. Cheap heads are churned out in only 3 to 4 days, but it takes Master carver Wang Yique a couple of weeks to give birth to his masterpieces…

Birth of a puppet

The article *Heads Up*, in Dragon Air's in-flight magazine, "The Silk Road," (September 1988) was about Quanzhou puppet master, Wang Yique, who at the time had made puppets for 60 years. Master Wang said, "I've done this since I was 13 years old. I can't give it up now. Besides, I want to leave something behind after I'm gone." He also noted that none of his children or grandchildren had chosen to make puppet heads.

Wang Yique spends up to half a month carving a head with exaggerated or distorted features that can be seen from a distance. Some puppets have four heads, 4 mouths and 8 eyes—all controllable by one finger!

Glove Puppet

Glove puppets appear simpler to use than marionettes, but these too require years of training. With the forefinger in the head, and thumb and middle finger operating the arms, the puppeteer can perform astonishing feats. The puppets pour tea into tiny pots, wield fans, change clothes, brandish swords, or perform somersaults while juggling barrels and dishes on poles balanced on their head. Quite literally breathtaking.

Quanzhou Puppet Troupe Museum. I could spend an entire day going through the endless displays of ancient and modern puppets ranging from warriors, emperors and the Monkey King and his entourage, to heroes of the Liberation, foreign villains, and musician puppets that play violins.

Address: No. 24 Tongzheng Lane, Quanzhou （泉州通政巷24号）

Amoymagic.com

Quanzhou Marionettes

Overseas Chinese History Museum (华侨历史博物) Given that most overseas Chinese hail from Southern Fujian (especially Quanzhou), it's no surprise the city has an extensive museum chronicling their history and their contributions to the motherland. The upper floor has an extensive

Overseas Chinese Museum

photo display of overseas Chinese' contributions to virtually every area of Quanzhou, particularly their financial contributions towards the renovation or construction of schools, hospitals, churches, temples, bridges—you name it, Overseas Chinese have a hand in it.

The Southern Shaolin Temple was rebuilt with the aid of 1 million Yuan from a Filipino Chinese and a Singaporean martial arts organization, and a Singaporean Chinese, Mr. Lin, gave 500,000 Yuan to build the Buddhist museum at Kaiyuan Temple.

Buddhist Museum (Kaiyuan Temple)

新加坡居仕林捐资50万元兴建佛教博物馆

Overseas Chinese' endless contributions have gone towards new schools, universities (like Yang En, New China's first private university), hospitals (Li Guo Xing gave 3 million Yuan for the emergency center), temples, churches, and perhaps most importantly in my eyes, roads.

Fish or Hook? "Better to give a man a hook and line than a fish," goes the saying, and the best hooks nowadays are new roads. A young friend of mine from Anxi lived a hard life of heavy labor in Xiamen for a decade, but saved enough money that he was able to plant fruit trees back home. The fruit would not have been worth harvesting a decade ago when poor mountain roads meant markets were four times as far. A couple years ago my friend said, "I'm going back home, Professor. Now I can make more money there than in Xiamen!"

Overseas Chinese' contributions to Quanzhou are endless!

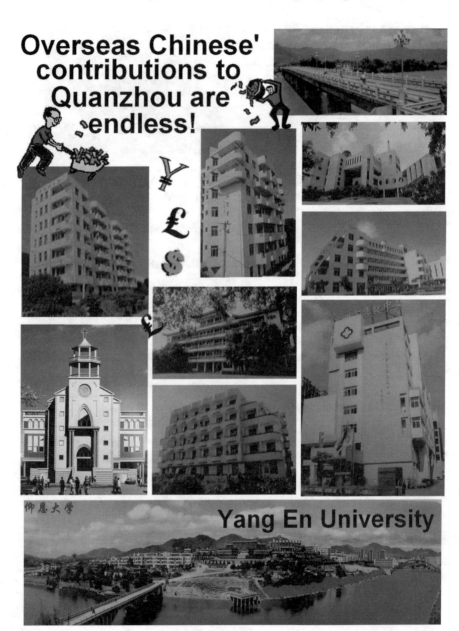

Yang En University

Pigs 'n Poison
The Overseas Chinese Museum also sheds light on a very dark subject—the notorious "Piggy Trade" (trafficking in coolies, which comes from the Chinese *kuli*,苦力, for "bitter labor."). Exhibits explain how we dastardly foreign-

Coolies packed for shipment

ers kidnapped Chinese and forced them to labor in inhuman conditions abroad. And, unfortunately, it is all too true. But...having said that, I think the museum should also note that the kidnapping itself was carried out by corrupt Chinese, who in turn sold them to dastardly foreigners. In the wax figure exhibit to the left, the boss beating the coolie was Chinese, not a foreigner. Granted, foreigners paid him—but that's my point.

"Coolie"
(Kuli)
"Bitter Labor"

Without the connivance of corrupt officials, the opium and coolie trades could never have survived—hence the article I wrote in People's Daily a few years back. China's greatest threat, now as then, is not direct foreign aggression but domestic corruption that allows us wily barbarians to get a foothold and then a stranglehold.

Hopefully, Laowai and Laonei alike will learn some lessons from the Poison 'n Piggy trades.

Getting There: (just west of Stadium, and East of Pizza Hut).
Hours: Inquire   **Phone**: 2987593

Other Miscellaneous City Sites

Tianfei Temple (天飞寺) Both Chinese and
foreign government officials and merchants used to
seek smooth sailing by offering sacrifices to the
Sea Goddess in Tianfei Temple (circa 1196).
Tianfe is nationally protected "History Museum for
Fujian-Taiwan Relations" has a large collection of
cultural relics, including the purported "Star of
David" (lying in the courtyard by a pile of assorted
relics).

**Miss Mazu
Sea goddess**

    Getting there: bus #24, or tourist bus #601
    Hours: 8:00 — 17:30   **Phone**: 220-3731

Two tales of Mazu and military folk...

Admiral Zheng He and the "Queen of Heaven"

    According to legend, when the Muslim admiral Zheng He
encountered a violent storm at sea, he calmed his passengers by
telling them the story of Miss Mazu. The storm abated, and upon
his return to China he asked the emperor to honor Mazu with a
royal title, whereupon the emperor declared her the "Queen of
Heaven," and built a temple for her.

General Lishang and Mazu

    When the Qing Dynasty General Lishang (in Nan' An chapter)
sailed to Taiwan to oust Koxinga's descendants, he took a Mazu
idol, which he left behind after his victory. He reported to the
Emperor how Miss Mazu had helped him gain victory, and the
Emperor gave her the title "Imperial Concubine," and ordered
Lishang to expand her temple on Meizhou island. As for the idol
left behind in Taiwan, over the centuries the smoke from countless worshippers' incense has turned Miss Mazu's face black, so
they've nicknamed her "Black-faced Mazu" (easier nicknaming
her than keeping her face clean, I suppose).

The Quanzhou Museum for Ancient Architecture (泉州古建筑博物馆)   Conveniently located downtown on the corner of Huxin St. and Wenling St., this museum is built on the site of the Hong Clan Ancestral Hall.   While you're in the area, stop at the Huxin Hotel for some of award-winning Chef Zhong's mouthwatering Quanzhou cuisine (check out the Quanzhou Cuisine chapter p.225).

Chengtian Temple
Amoymagic.com

Chengtian Temple (承天寺), on Nanjunxiang Lane (南俊巷), is one of Quanzhou's three greatest Buddhist Temples (the other two being Kaiyuan and Chongfu).   It was first built in the Tang Dynasty, and renovated in the 30th year of Emperor Kangxi in the Qing Dynasty.   (That's 1691 A.D., for us foreigners).   The brochure says it used to have "ten wonderful views" but was renovated and returned to its original condition (which means, I suppose, that the original did not have the 10 wonderful views?).

Getting there: Bus # 19, Bus # 16, Bus # 18, Bus # 25.
Hours: 6:00 — 17:30   **Phone**: 227-6917

Chongfu Temple (崇福寺)   This recently renovated temple on Chongfu Road (崇福路) is a provincial level protected cultural relic, and where Shaolin Kungfu was taught after Quanzhou's Shaolin Temple was destroyed.   Be sure and visit the reconstructed Southern Shaolin Temple on the hill behind the Sports Stadium(p.90) .

Chongfu Temple
(Part of Quanzhou's
S. Shaolin Heritage)
Amoymagic.com

Getting there: Bus #15
Hours: 6:00 — 17:30   **Phone**: 278-4046

Zaytun Street Life

"Many come hither from Upper India to have their bodies painted with the needle in the way we have elsewhere described, there being many adepts at this craft in the city [Zaytun]"

Marco Polo

Pavilion by Night

It's no wonder that medieval travelers claimed Zaytun was intoxicating. If you wanted it, Quanzhou had it—everything from silken tapestries to tattoos. While Quanzhou is tamer nowadays, there's still enough to keep you busy--especially at night, when bright lights are strung through the trees, and across buildings and pagodas. Night markets are a shopper's paradise (and her husband's nightmare), offering everything imaginable and a few things that aren't. And street vendors' endlessly diverse offerings of snacks are guaranteed to please your stomach as well as your wallet.

Fortune Tellers

A key enterprise

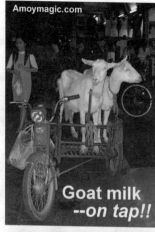

Roasted chestnuts

Goat milk
--*on tap!!*

Streetside artist

Sue cottons to
cotton candy

Time flies when you're being had

"His music isn't as bad as it sounds." Mark Twain (of Wagner).

Each evening, rain or shine, local artists perform music or drama on stages set up by intersections. Others sketch charcoal caricatures, or transform names into beautiful works of calligraphy. And there is always a fellow who weaves amazingly realistic flowers and insects from leaves, and

Nightly streetside performances

sells them for a pittance to locals and tourists alike. The streets are one

unending delightful performance. And if in spite of all this revelry you find yourself down in the dumps—try visiting the dumps…

Hui'an Maidens?

Supplement

Down in the Dumps?

No, I'm not really suggesting you visit the city dump or sightsee the sewage treatment center, but they are in fact remarkable, and part of the reason that Quanzhou has been able to balance mushrooming economic growth with preservation of its historical, cultural and natural heritage. And in an age when environmental problems loom large over us (especially in China, with 1.3 billion consumers/disposers), it's encouraging to see cities like Quanzhou that make preservation of their environment a priority.

Passing Water [1] Quanzhou treats only 30% of its daily sewage, but that's better than 0% a decade ago, and new plants should get the city to 80% by 2010. The 133 million Yuan Baozhou Sewage Treatment Plant is state-of-the art, and treated water is pure

Treated Sewage used in waterfall and fish pond

enough that it can be used for irrigation or, as in this photo I took, to raise fish!

Down in the Dumps Quanzhou has one of China's most advanced volume-reduced, harmless sanitary landfills. It easily meets present needs, and a new plant is being built for future demands. The plant not only uses the most cutting edge imported technology and practices but also employs some good old Chinese ingenuity—like lining the dumping grounds with inert waste from the shoe industry.

---

[1] Sign in restaurant of Acapulco, Mexico's 5-Star Princess Hotel: "The manager has personally passed all of the water."

This gets rid of the waste, and also forms an additional protection against percolating liquids. Fascinating, eh? Or maybe not—but it's these kinds of practices behind-the-scenes that make the Quanzhou that tourists see such a beautiful, clean and healthy place to visit. And its getting better. Phase Two will improve recycling, and allow conversion of some waste into fertilizer. This, combined with extensive campaigns to encourage citizens to reduce, reuse and recycle, and to presort garbage, are all part of Quanzhou's holistic planning, and a good reason why the City of Light may still be around when less enlightened cities have gone the way of the dodo bird.

Notes

[1] "Unforgettable Journey—Fifty Years for Fujian Christian Churches on the Three-Self," published by "The Three Self-Patriotic Movement Committee of Christian Churches in Fujian and the Fujian Christian Council."

[2] Rev. Carstairs Douglas, who did more for Westerner's understanding of the Minnan Dialect than perhaps any other man, was in excellent health one day and dead of virulent cholera the next. Talmadge wrote of Douglas,

"By overwork he had worn himself out, and made himself an old man while he was yet comparatively young in years. He came to China quite young and at the time of his death was only about forty-six years of age, and yet men who had recently become acquainted with him thought him over sixty... he did more work during the twenty-two years of his missionary life than most men accomplish in twice that time..."

"Recently, especially during the last year, it was manifest, at least to others, that his physical strength was fast giving way. Yet he could not be prevailed upon to leave his field for a season for temporary rest, or even to lessen the amount of his work.

"I never knew a more incessant worker. He was a man of most extensive general information. I think I have never met with his equal in this respect. He was acquainted with several modern European languages and was a thorough student of the original languages of Holy Scripture, as witness the fact of his study of the Hebrew Bible, even after his last sickness had commenced. As regards the Chinese language, he was already taking his place among the first sinologues of the land."

[3] Pitcher, Rev. Philip Wilson, "In and About Amoy," Methodist Publishing House in China, Shanghai and Foochow, 1912., p. 283

Chapter 4

Quanzhou Outskirts

Quanzhou Shaolin Temple (泉州少林寺)
It seems every village in Fujian makes three claims: 1) tastiest food, 2) prettiest girls, and 3) deadliest Kungfu (preceding adjectives not necessarily in that order). Each village has its own traditions, passed down only to those who share the

Quanzhou S. Shaolin Temple
(Photo courtesy of Abbot Shi)

same surname, but supposedly all Southern Shaolin Kungfu originated right here in Quanzhou's Shaolin Temple! (Fujian's Putian and Fuqing make the same claim, but 1,000 years ago Putian was part of Quanzhou anyway).

Quanzhou's Shaolin Temple is behind the Sports Stadium at the very end of Zaytun St. (Citong Rd., 刺桐路，on Dongyue Hill (东岳山). It is exactly 1.1 km past the sign that says you only have 600 meters to go. I mentioned this to the abbot of the temple, and asked if it meant 600 meters if you

600 meters = 1.1 kilometers?

climb straight up. He said, "No, Kungfu monks fly straight up!"

Quanzhou Southern Shaolin temple was built in the early Tang Dynasty by the monk Zhikong, who had moved here from the Songshan Shaolin Temple up north. The temple had its ups and downs and eventually was totally destroyed in 1763 A.D.. The Shaolin tradition continued to be taught in Chongfu Temple (p.83), but now that so many folks around the world are getting their kicks out of Kungfu, the Shaolin temple was recently rebuilt. Each year, thousands of Kungfu enthusiasts, make pilgrimages to this Mecca for martial arts enthusiasts and also visit the martial arts schools and museum(p.94).

Kungfu Architecture   Notice the trimmings and carvings under the temple eaves. Unlike other temples, they all depict Southern Shaolin monks in different fighting postures.

Abbot Shi Changding   I'd have never imagined a 30-year-old like Master Shi Changding (释常定) could be abbot of S. Shaolin Temple! (Costello, maybe, but not abbot).   Since he began kungfu at age 13, Master Shi has made a name for himself, and helped put Quanzhou's S. Shaolin Temple back on the map.   The young abbot is also a Wushu Colonel, assistant secretary-general of Quanzhou Wushu association, adviser to the France-Fujian martial arts association, and people's conference representative.   He has helped initiate many international exchange programs with martial arts groups and

Abbot Shi Changding

organizations throughout Asia, Europe and the Americas.   Now Master Shi has set his sites on expanding the Southern Shaolin Complex.

Contact Master Shi at: Shaolin Temple, Dong Yue Mountain,
      Quanzhou City, Fujian, P.R. of China, 362000
      中国福建泉州市东岳山少林寺 362000
      Phone: (0595)279-5119.

Getting to S. Shaolin Temple: Bus #7, #10, #11, #13, #19
      Hours: 6:00 — 22:00   **Phone**: 279-5119

泉州少林寺简介及规划图

An American Delegation

Abbot Shi receiving a French martial artist

Thai Students
(Photo Courtesy of Abbot Shi)

(Photo Courtesy of Abbot Shi)

Abbot Shi in Paris
(Photo Courtesy of Abbot Shi)

(Photo Courtesy of Abbot Shi)

Southern Shaolin Kungfu Museum

(泉州南少林武术博物馆)

You'll get lots of kicks out of the Wushu (martial arts) hall of Quanzhou Sports Center. The four key exhibits are:

1. "Shaolin Wushu Handed on from Ancient Times and Developed in Quanzhou."
2. "Heyday of Shaolin Giving Birth to a Multitude of Heroes."
3. "Carry Forth the Good Tradition and Let 100 Flowers Blossom." (I suggested adding a "Let 100 Lawnmowers Follow" annex).
4. "Make Friends with Wushu and Let the Seeds of Friendship Spread All Over the World."

(Photo courtesy of Abbot Shi)

Stone Bamboo (石笋) Just outside the city's western wall, sometime before 1011 A.D., someone erected the 4.18 meter high "stone bamboo shoot." But given the totem was the object of fertility worship (生殖崇拜, shengzhi chongbai), I suspect that "bamboo shoot" is just a euphemism for the biological appendage that it closely resembles (though a bit big, granted). To make sure I did not miss the allusion, my companion exclaimed, "The shoot is aligned with those two hills. See? They're the breasts! Can you tell?"

I wasn't ready to make a clean breast of things so I kept quiet (yes, it does happen!).

Stone Bamboo Shoot

Ye Olde Breasts

Fertility totems are still used in Thailand, where new brides rub against them to insure they have a baby boy. I don't know if it works or not, but given China's 1.3 billion population, I'd think they would barricade this particular bamboo shoot.

As I gazed at the stone bamboo shoot, I could not help but pity the panda that comes across it. Pretty tough on the teeth. And I was reminded of the panda that paid his tab in a bar, pulled out a pistol, shot out the lights, and headed for the door. When the bartender cried out, "Why on earth did you do that?" the panda said, "I'm a panda bear. Look it up."

Like any good bartender he kept a dictionary under the counter so he pulled it out, looked up "panda," and read, "Panda: Chinese bear; eats shoots and leaves."

Qingyuan Mountain (清源山)   After the Maritime Museum, Kaiyuan Temple, and puppets, next on my list is Qingyuan Mountain. Just 2.5 km north of the city, this is not only a beautiful place (called "Fujian's Fairy Land") but also a holy site for many religions, including Buddhism, Taoism, and Tibetan Buddhism.

Qingyuan (Clear Water) Mountain is the perfect destination when someone tells you to go take a hike. Secluded and silent, save for the sound of waterfalls and gurgling brooks, the densely wooded trails wind past pagodas, temples, and 36 caves. Pilgrims used to worship the hundreds of statues in the caves until the Red Guard destroyed the relics. Now visitors worship empty holes, perhaps because they are holey.

Qingyuan's amazing collection of religious relics ranges from "Old Stone Saint," (老君岩), China's largest Taoist statue (see below) to the statues of 3 Tibetan Buddhist Lamas (三世佛) in Bixiao Cave (they were thought to be Buddhas until the outer layer of concrete was removed). The Manichaean who founded Cao'an Monastery, the planet's last Manichaean temple, is buried on Qingyuan, though no one knows where.

Before (Buddhas) *and* After (Tibetan Lamas!)

Other popular Qingyuan Mtn. sites include the statue of a seated Avalokitesvara, beside the Thousand Hand Rocks, a statue of Sakyamuni inside Niche Cavern (on the left peak), and the tomb of Hong Yi. One of the best views of Quanzhou City is from "South Platform Rock." And you can reach all of these sites easily and safely, thanks to endless trails laid out by centuries of nature lovers and devotees of various religions who have laid out paths and steps—lots of steps!

Steps   On his last trip to Quanzhou, Alan Smith, founder of Nations in Bloom, mopped his perspiring brow and said, "Chinese steps only go up—never down!"

Over the past 5,105 years, Chinese have built steps up every hillside and mountain in China. No doubt, even Mount Everest has steps on the Chinese side, and Tibetans at the top sell mineral water, roasted water melon seeds, and peanuts.

Many is the time I've imagined myself to be the first to hike some remote hill, only to stumble across granite steps worn smooth by time and tourists. But on the bright side—it's not likely that hikers in China can ever get lost.

Ancient Escalator?

Old Stone Saint (老君岩)   The Song Dynasty Old Stone Saint ("#1 Laozi Under Heaven!") is China's oldest Taoist sculpture, and the largest (5.1 m. high by 7.3 m. wide). Legend claims that if you rub his nose you'll live 120 years; rub his eye and you'll reach 160. Folks used to say

you'd die early if you rubbed his mouth, but such down in the mouth talk didn't exactly bolster tourism, so now locals brightly mouth off, "Rub mouth, get good luck!" Alas, 1,000 years of rubbing Lao Tzu the wrong way was rubbing his nose away, so a few years back they fenced him off and hired a guard so no else can take Lao Zi for granite.

Getting There: Bus#3, # 5, #20, or Special Tourist Bus #601
Hours: 5:30 — 16:00   **Phone**: 278-3474

Qingyuan Mountain

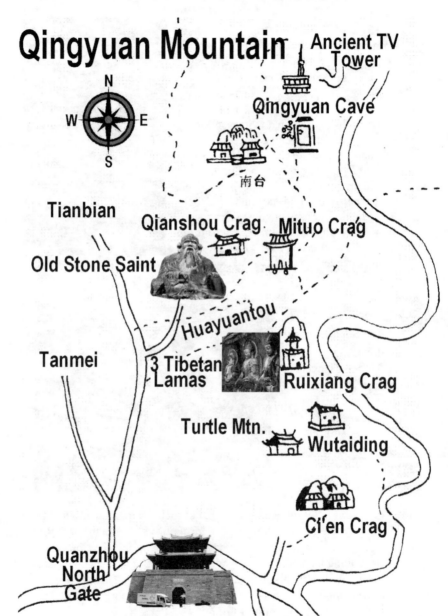

Ancient TV Tower

Qingyuan Cave

南台

Tianbian

Qianshou Crag

Mituo Crag

Old Stone Saint

Huayuantou

Tanmei

3 Tibetan Lamas

Ruixiang Crag

Turtle Mtn.

Wutaiding

Ci'en Crag

Quanzhou North Gate

Muslim Zaytun
Ibn Battuta

"The Muslims live in a town apart from the others.

"On the day that I reached Zaytun I saw there the amir who had come to India as an envoy with the present [to the sultan], and who afterwards traveled with our party and was shipwrecked on the junk. He greeted me, and introduced me to the controller of the douane and saw that I was given good apartments [there]. I received visits from the qadi of the Muslims, the shaykh al-Islam, and the principal merchants. Amongst the latter was Sharaf ad-Din of Tabriz, one of the merchants from whom I had borrowed at the time of my arrival in India, and the one who had treated me most fairly. He knew the Koran by heart and used to recite it constantly. These merchants, living as they do in a land of infidels, are overjoyed when a Muslim comes to them. They say "He has come from the land of Islam," and they make him the recipient of the tithes on their properties, so that he becomes as rich as themselves. There was living at Zaytun, amongst other eminent shaykhs, Burhan ad-Din of Kazarun, who has a hermitage outside the town, and it is to him that the merchants pay the sums they vow to Shaykh Abu Ishaq of Kazarun."

"Holy Tombs" (灵山伊斯兰教圣墓)   A Ming Dynasty Stele in the Fuzhou Mosque's courtyard (behind two rusty bicycles) claims Mohammed sent 4 disciples to China between 618 A.D. - 626 A.D.. One went to Guangzhou, one to Yangzhou, and two settled in Quanzhou.   Sashye

Entrance to "Holy Hill"

(Sa-ke-zu—the 3rd Saint) and Gaoshi (Wu-ko-su—the 4th Saint) were buried on the east edge of town, past the Maritime Museum, on "Holy Hill."

Holy Tombs

This very grave site was called "Holy Hill" because after the disciples' burial, villagers encountered supernatural signs on the hill (the hillside glowed at night, for instance).

Some say China's first

Muslims were not in Quanzhou but Chang'an, the ancient capital, in 650 A.D.. But the tombs' spindle-shaped granite columns are Tang Dynasty—at least 1,000 years old, so they're ancient, regardless of who rests there, and they have been revered for a millennium. Furthermore, Mohammed is reputed to have said, "Seek knowledge, as far as China," so when his persecuted followers fled to Africa, it is likely some came to China as well (along with the Manicheans and Nestorians).

1322 Renovation. An Arabic inscription on a granite stele records the tombs' restoration in 1322. Part of it says, in effect, that Quanzhou Moslems

"...renovated this blessed Tomb, with the purpose of pleasing the most noble and majestic Allah and obtaining rich rewards from him... the two saints came to China in the time of Faghfur. They were reported to be men of high virtue. After their deaths, they passed from this incorruptible world into everlasting eternity. People believe in them in the hope of obtaining their benediction. Once in trouble or caught between two fires, they approach the Tomb begging for enlightenment by offering sacrifice. In so doing, they always obtain what they come for and return home in peace."[1]

Arabic recounting renovation in 1322 A.D.

Admiral Zheng He's Pilgrimage Another slab records the visit of the great Muslim Chinese mariner Zheng He, who visited the tombs in 1417 before his 5th voyage, in which he also visited Mecca. After Zheng He departed, the local magistrate erected a monument to the event. It read,

Record of Zhenghe's visit in 1417 A.D.

"The imperial envoy, commander-in-chief and eunuch Zheng He, is going to the country Hormuz and other countries across the sea, and made a pilgrimage to this Holy Tomb to crave the blessings and protection of the saints on the 16th of the 5th month in the 15th year of Yongle (May 30th, 1417 A.D.)."

[1] The Islamic Historic Relics in Quanzhou, Fujian People's Publishing House

Zheng He offered sacrifices and prayed for safety (a common practice even with Muslims then). Whether prayers helped or not, Zheng He sailed most of the known world--and, incidentally, helped spread Islam throughout Southeast Asia.

Muslims don't monopolize Holy Hill, which also has Buddhist tombs scattered about, but the Muslims are taking back the territory. An army of stone masons, directed by architects armed with intricate sketches, is building dozens of new Muslim tombs (most for the "Ding" clan—the primary clan in Chendai Village).

Muslim very Grave Site

Windrocking Stone (风动石) As
your guide leads you down the garden
path to the tombs, on the right you'll the
famous "windrocking stone," inscribed
with large Chinese characters meaning
"Wonder of Nature." Zhou Daoguang,
a Ming Dynasty official, visited the
stone, dubbed it Jaspar Ball, and carved

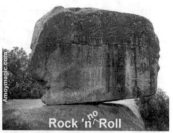
Rock 'n' Roll

an inscription on the rock. Considered one of Quanzhou's "Top Eight
Spectacular Sights," its claim to fame is that it "sways gently with the
wind and moves with a mere touch of the hand." My hosts said it was a
"gift of Allah," rivaling the "Swaying Tower of Esfahan."[2]

Chinese have even written poems about the great wonder of nature:
> "The ball of a stone sways and sways above the lake,
> and was christened the Purple Platform by Prefect the late.
> The wintry moon from celestial palace gate emerges,
> Shooting stars shower like beads on the bronze plate of earth.
> A flowing stream swift as an arrow turns the sakya wheel,
> Which looks the look of a mirror round from the
> Far Ball Hill.
> Oft-time hear the shrill cries of cranes pass the sky;
> Leisurely the fairies dawdle away their time and tide."

"It's good luck to move this stone!" a Moslem said. "It moves easily
for the pure of heart." Well, that's me! So I placed a fingertip on it, and
then a palm, an arm, my entire body—it did not budge. We finally
wedged a stick under it, balanced a cell phone on the stick, and in unison
three of us shoved—and the cell phone shook a little. "See! See!"

Blessed are the pure in heart.

There is also a sweet spring trickling from beneath the stone—but it
apparently dried up at my approach. I didn't even see mud.
Getting There: Buses 7,10,11,13,19,23,25
Hours: 8:00 — 17:30   **Phone**: 210-1631

---

[2] In Esfahan, Iran, if either of the minarets flanking the tomb of Amu
Abdollah (died 1316 A.D.) is shaken, the other minaret shakes as well.

Water God Temple
(Zhenwu Temple at Fashi,
法石镇武寺）Since the
Song Dynasty, locals have
worshipped Xianwu, the
Water God, as well as
offered sacrifices to the
sea god, in this Shitou
Street Temple. Even with
rivers on both sides of the
city, water has not always
been easy to come by, as
evident from the local
legend below...

Water God Temple

> **Getting There**: Buses #1, 5, 21
> **Hours**: 6:00 — 17:30

God Gives Rain to xichuan—A Local Legend

A 1,000 years ago, Quanzhou suffered such a severe drought
that everyone, from the Mayor on down, was praying for water.
An angel passing by on his way West to Sichuan took pity on
Quanzhou, but told officials, "I regret I cannot help. God has
told me to bring rain to Sichuan, and if I release it here instead
he will be angry."

"No problem,"said an official. "We will rename this area
"xichuan" [using a different "si"], and you can give us the rain
and still tell god you took the rain to Sichuan." The angel
agreed, and in appreciation, locals erected a "xichuan
pavilion" on the south end of Luoyang Bridge, and it stands to
this day."(photo on p.118)

And now, Quanzhou Parks…

Supplement

Traveling Out of Town

After the next chapter (on Quanzhou Parks), we head for Quanzhou's rural countries. Fortunately, roads are better than Beaton's "new roads" in 1945. In fact, they're a lot better than way back in 1995, when it took me over 30 hours to drive to Wuyi Mountain (now it takes only nine).

"New roads make traveling easier..."
(Beaton, 1945)

Reverend Pitcher, in "In and about Amoy," wrote:

"Traveling in the Amoy district is a slow process, more often wearisome than otherwise,—a peculiar wearisomeness of its own."

"So far as South China is concerned there are no roads. The nearest approach to a road, generally speaking, is a narrow footpath, something like the cow paths that lead to our meadows, winding and twisting like some serpent among the paddy (rice fields). These paths are raised about a foot above the fields, and were originally made so as to mark the divisional lines between the property of different owners.

"The only commissioner of these highways is the tramp of ceaseless thousands bearing their heavy burdens over them, from one generation to another. One never expects them to be kept in good order. No fences mark their boundary, no sign-posts point their direction. The stranger easily becomes confused and lost among boundless fields covered with a network of paths that seem to run in every direction but the right one."

Pitcher, *In and About Amoy*, 1912, p.265

Chapter 5
Quanzhou Gardens & Parks

Ibn Battuta remarked upon Quanzhou people's love of gardens and nature, and judging from the number of parks and natural preserves, gardens are still their first love.

Micro to Macro Gardening   Quanzhou is like a four-tiered miniature landscape. It starts with the prize-winning miniature gardens that common folk throughout the city grow in their courtyards or on balconies, and expands to residential gardens, community parks and squares, city gardens, and finally parks and forests that include the surrounding mountains and rivers.

Community parks, squares and forests reflect the harmony, creativity and care invested in potted landscapes—but on a much larger scale. Between 1992 and 2002, Quanzhou spent 40 million USD establishing 358.3 hectares of unique gardens, ranging from Eastern Lake Park to Quanzhou Forest Park.   With land at a premium, they've had to be pretty innovative—like building car parks below kid parks, or using "vertical" landscaping (rooftop gardens, hanging planters).

Each park is unique. West Lake "tea boats" offer unique views of the island bird sanctuary. Quanzhou Water Park attracts vacationers. Kaiyuan Temple offers serenity, and Fuxin Garden Square has a musical fountain. Qingyuan Mountain, the ancient "Fairyland," appeals to both athletes and meditative types, who enjoy the Taoist setting. Some parks have entrance charges to cover maintenance costs, but where possible parks are inexpensive or free to maximize use by low-income families

Bridging the Gap   With the growing generation gap, Quanzhou is seeking innovative ways to meet the needs of both young and old by emphasizing both passive and active leisure and cultural activities, educational activities for retirees, and increased opportunities for elderly volunteers. City parks offer the older generation plenty of opportunities to teach the youth Chinese shadow boxing, calligraphy, Chinese painting, or how to perform the simple but elegant Minnan tea ceremony.

West Lake Park (西 湖 公 园) Every decent sized city in China has a West Lake Park (the most famous being that in Hangzhou). But Quanzhou's newly renovated park is a beauty.

Called "Northwest Ocean" by locals, this park lies in the northwest of the city, and was a swamp until the city dredged it out. Dykes and bridges connect the islands, which have once again become home to wild creatures and birds. Ornately painted wooden pleasure boats serve tea as you are given the lake tour. Take a camera to

Serving Tea on a West Lake Boat

photograph the wild pigeons and egrets, which sometimes almost cover the trees. Also visit the many memorial forests planted by Quanzhou volunteers.

    Getting There: Buses #3,15,17,21, and 27
    Hours: 8:00 — 17:30   **Phone**: 289-5875

East Lake Park (东湖公园)   The nicely wooded and landscaped East Lake Park, right in the middle of town, was one of Quanzhou's original "Eight Famous Sites." Scenes surrounding the "Lotus Fragrance on the Stars" lake include, Fragrance of Lotus, Pavilion of Praying for Plain Wind, and Children's Playground.

    Getting There: Buses 1,2,7,11,13,17,20,22
    Hours: 8:00 — 17:30   **Phone**: 2280147

Zaytun Park (刺桐公园)   Zaytun Park (Citong Park), on Zaytun Road, was opened in 1997. Official sites include "Citong Sunken Flowerbed," "Listening to Rain in Banana Groves," deng deng and more deng.
    Getting There: Bus 22A or 23
    Hours: 8:00 — 17:30   **Phone**: 2578935

Fragrant Grass Garden (苏草园)   This delightful midtown garden on Xinmen Street was built by General Shilang, and was the location of the original Chongzheng Academy.
    Getting there: Buses 4,6,25,26
    Hours: 8:00 — 17:30   **Phone**: 238-2838

Water World (**Aquatic Elysium,** 泉州水上乐园**, Shuishang Le-yuan**)
This park is a real hit with our family because its big (47,357 m2!), fun, and very inexpensive—such a bargain that during summers we load up Toy Ota with a dozen kids, drive to Water World from Xiamen, and drive back late that evening. We like the water slides, paddle boats, and tidal pool (though I've had bigger waves in our bathtub).

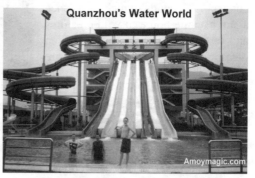
Quanzhou's Water World

Water World's sole drawback is that, like stores and shopping centers, there is no respite from nonstop 200 decibel Chinese pop music blasting from speakers strung up every 10 feet. Wax ear plugs, maybe?

After a nice wet day, order a pizza and build a towering salad in one of Quanzhou's Pizza Huts, then head home on the new Quanzhou-Xiamen Toll-way to recover from your sunburn.   Or else head north to Luoyang Bridge (we give Fujian's excellent Bridges a chapter of their own!).
    Getting There: 3,15,17, and 27
    Hours: 8:00 — 22:00 (during season)   **Phone**: 277-6005

Quanzhou Amuse-ment Center (泉州游乐园) is in Quanzhou Exhibition Town, just south of Quanzhou across the river. The English brochure boasts it covers more than 250 mu. Moo.

The 30+ amusements include the ferris wheel, roller coaster, playground, and go-karts. To quote the brochure, "It is a large modern playground integrating amusement, shopping and bodybuild."   I'm sold!

Getting There: Buses 9,18,23,25 and special tourist bus #601
Hours: 8:00 — 20:00   **Phone**: 248-1835

Parks in Rural Quanzhou

Anxi Zhimin Field Sport and Ecological Recreation Center (安溪志闽野外运动生态游乐中心)   Wow—now that is a mouthful!
This outdoors center in Anxi's Longmen Township offers a good day or two of exciting outdoor activities, including white water rafting (supposedly the best in Fujian!), rock-climbing, hunting, hiking, field survival, and tea making (which can be as arduous as the rest).

Getting There: Bus to Anxi, change buses to Longmen Town
Hours: All Day   **Phone**: 3318787

Dehua Peach Fairy Creek Ecological Tourist Area (德化桃仙生态旅游区)   Peach Fairy Creek (Taoxian Xi) offers bamboo rafting, rubber rafting, hiking, and traditional performances of Nanyin (Southern Music), Folk songs, and Santong Drum (三通鼓).

Getting There: Bus to Dehua, changes buses to Nancheng Town.
Hours: 8:00 — 17:30   **Phone**: 3618888

Every Home a Garden?   About 700 years ago, the Arab traveler Ibn Battuta remarked upon Quanzhou people's love of gardening, and that love of nature is still seen today, ranging from the intimate care given miniature landscapes and balcony plants to neighborhood gardens, community parks, and city parks and forests. Gardening is a grassroots affair, from the bottom up as well as top down.   And Quanzhou folks' aesthetics have transferred to architecture as well.

Garden Architecture   Most Chinese cities' approach to rapid modernization seem to be to raze everything old and replace it with tile- and glass-covered concrete cubicles. (Of course, who are we Americans to talk?   We don't have ancient culture to preserve, but we do have a natural heritage, which we're decimating. New housing developments invariably begin with bulldozing down the ancient trees, which are then replaced with saplings bought on sale at a local nursery).

Quanzhou's marriage of old and new architecture accommodates not only the natural heritage but the cultural and historical heritage as well. The new housing areas are a delightful blend of old and new, retaining the ancient Chinese or foreign flavor, while incorporating modern technology and

"Kid Park above, Car Park below!"

innovations such as solar water heating.   And while the first new apartment buildings had little in the way of green space, Quanzhou leaders have a motto, "Do more, learn more," and each successive project has had more, and better, greenery (thanks in part to innovations like car parks below gardens.

Today, as in Marco Polo's day, Quanzhou's true wealth lies not in products but the place, and the people.

Protected Trees Amidst
"New Classic" Architecture

Garden Architecture

Zaytun's Walls Rise Again!

Downtown Project

Before

Ancient Minnan Architecture, Hi-Tech Solar Heating

and...

After!

Shopping Area Near Ashab Mosque

New Residential District

New Apartment Building

Chapter 6

Quanzhou Bridges

"Central Fujian bridges are second to none under heaven"
Chinese saying

"The bridges of China are wonders! On some of them people build their temples and houses and shops—where they live and carry on their business. There are at least two bridges of this kind in the Amoy district, each having a population of from fifty to one hundred inhabitants—perhaps more. These bridges are generally of wonderful construction. How the largest of them were built must always remain a matter of pure conjecture.

"Twenty-five miles west of Amoy there is a famous bridge...There are natives who will tell you that man could not have lifted, by any imaginable machinery, to their present position those immense stones of which it is made. The only conclusion they can come to is, the gods must have done the work.

"The bridge is called 'The Po-lam Bridge'—a place much frequented by foreigners residing in Amoy. It is 200 yards or more long, built upon solid stone piers each about twelve feet high. Some of the stones laid on these piers are of great length and weight. One of them is seventy feet long, five feet thick and four feet wide, weighing something like 107 tons. It always has been a question: How were they put in place?"
Pitcher, *In and About Amoy*, 1912, p.297~8

Land of Bridges   Quanzhou is a land of bridges, both literally and metaphorically. Zaytun was not only the bridge between China and the rest of the planet (assuming they were on the same planet), but it also gave us some of the world's most unique bridges, spanning rivers, gorges, and bays. Given our vertical province's tortuous topography, it is no wonder that Quanzhou folk excelled in bridge-making. By the Song Dynasty, Minnan alone had at least 313 bridges.

My favorite bridges include the magnificent 700-year-old wooden covered bridge in Pingnan, Putian's Ninggai Bridge (which is protected by a modern bridge built right over top), and Quanzhou's magnificent Anping Bridge (longest stone bridge on earth) and Luoyang Bridge.

My Favorite Fujian Bridges

Before visiting Quanzhou's mythic bridges, view them through the eyes of Ms. Averil Mackenzie-Grieve, a resident of South Fujian in the 1920s:

> "Galeote Pereira, when he was captured by the Chinese as a smuggler in 1549, was taken through Ch'uan-chou [Quanzhou] on his way to Foochow, and was greatly impressed with the populous countryside, the 'gallantly paved streets' and, above all, 'the very noble and very well-wrought bridges of stone…for service over the rivers'. Ch'uan-chou's bridge was even more splendid that Foochow's bridge of Ten Thousand Ages, surpassed only by the one spanning the Loyang river ten miles to the north. For me, the great granite bridges of Fukien had an indescribable fascination. It lay, not in their uniqueness (there are believed to be none like them in the world), but, I think, in the grand, brave way in which they spanned the rivers, set their broad buttresses against the currents. Their grey bulk had personality and inspired respect; they reminded me of elephants. No one knows exactly how the stones were put into place. The buttresses supported solid granite slabs twenty-two feet long, two feet thick, laid, in the bridge over the Loyang estuary, five abreast for over a thousand feet. At the roofed gateway sat a massive stone figure, the twelfth-century builder himself. When we saw them, their function had not altered in any way since they had been built.
>
> "For me, the Roman coliseum rises yawning like an empty wasps' nest; life has gone from it. Even in Lucca, whose coliseum is a teeming hive of cell-slums, built with the help of Lombardic bricks and Romanesque hewn stones, builders and users are buried in history—remembered it is true, but as a legend. But across the great stone Fukienese bridges the people swarmed, thinking, acting, writing, talking, exactly as their forebears had done for more than seven hundred years. The stream of pole-carriers, litter-bearers, pedestrians, flowed unbroken throughout the centuries, the strong tide of life undiminished, undiluted; an endurance so close-textured, so ubiquitous that, living in China, one accepted it and only afterwards was amazed."
>
> (Excerpt from, *A Race of Green Ginger*, p.112,113)

Quanzhou's three most famous bridges are Luoyang Bridge, Anping Bridge, and Dongguan Bridge. Dongguan, in Yongchun, is a bit off the beaten path, so we'll visit it after we've seen two marvelous bridges just off the 324 national highway.

Anping Bridge (安平桥)

This recently renovated 2,251m bridge was the longest bridge on earth during the Middle Ages, and is still the longest stone bridge today. It was built in 1138 in Anhai by the monk Zupai as a replacement for the ferry, and wasn't completed until 1151. He used massive granite slabs, most of which are said to have been shipped from nearby Jinmen Island (Quemoy). It was originally called the Five Mile Bridge because it was Five Li (Chinese Miles) long—but I'm not sure if they were the long li, short li, mandarin li or common country li. Whichever li, the bridge is a long walk on a hot summer day, so take it slowli.

Luoyang Bridge(洛阳桥)

To the north of Quanzhou city lies China's first seaport bridge, the Luoyang Bridge. Though shorter than Anping, it is older—and my favorite by far.

Before Mr. Cai Xiang (1012—1067) was able to overcome incredible difficulties to erect the Luoyang Bridge, traversing the Luoyang river required travelers to spend an entire day going inland, or to chance crossing on small craft that were often sunk by squalls sent by evil spirits. In 1053, Quanzhou prefect Cai Xiang, who was born in Xianyou and became a Jinshi at the tender age of 19, decided to remedy the situation by building a stone bridge at the mouth of the Luoyang River.

Mr. Caixiang

Mr. Cai Xiang used many innovative engineering techniques, including what may be one of the planet's first biological engineering. The piers were ingeniously shaped like a ship's bow to divert the raging tides. Chinese, always poetic, call them "10,000 ships launching." (They miscounted by 9,900 but that's "liway",

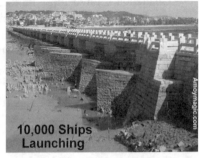

10,000 Ships Launching

remember). The pillars' massive granite blocks were held together with butterfly-shaped iron wedges (hence the origin of "Iron Butterfly"—almost 400 years after Kaiyuan Temple's "Purple Haze"). The pillars were further reinforced with live oysters, whose natural secretions cemented the blocks together. (I asked my guides how they trained the oysters to cooperate but they clammed up on me).

The granite slabs were up to 10 meters long and one meter wide, and weighed ten tons. Each time I traverse the bridge, I marvel that the ancients could have even hewn the mammoth blocks, much less transported them to the Luoyang River, where they battled its legendarily ferocious currents to set them in place.

Amóymagic.com

Historical records relate that the completed bridge was 834 meters long by 7 meters wide, and had 500 stone sculptures to serve as railings, all supported upon 46 piers (talk about pier pressure!). Over 700 pine trees were planted on both ends of the bridge, and as further protection from typhoons, the bridge was armed with 28 stone lions, 7 pavilions, 9 towers, and numerous stone warriors.

A Border Stone in the middle bears the characters Jin-Hui Jiaojiang because the center of the bridge lay on the border between Hui'an and Jinjiang.

Border Stone

The bridge stood largely unchanged for centuries. Even during the 8.0 earthquake almost 400 years ago (which toppled Ashab Mosque's dome), the bridge suffered only minor damage. But Japanese invaders accomplished what nature could not. In the center of the bridge is a Pusa that used to have a moonstone in her forehead. It supposedly glowed at night, guiding seamen to safety—until the Japanese stole it.

Moonstoneless Pusa

1 Million Yuan Renovation! Luoyang bridge was renovated several times after 1949. The renovation in the early 90s cost over 1 million Yuan. When I asked why it was so costly, an official said, "Because nowadays we have to dig away half a mountain to find a ten meter slab of granite!"

Maybe they could try shorter pieces and lots more oysters?

Cai Xiang Memorial Temple, (蔡襄祠, Cai Xiang Ci), is south of Luoyang Bridge. Within is a stone tablet, "The Records of Building Wan'An Bridge," inscribed by the great bridge builder himself. "Wan 'An" (10,000 Peace) was another popular name for Luoyang bridge.

Buddha's buttocks?

Making Waves   One large sunbaked stone has a natural formation resembling a snake and a turtle head. It is said that before the bridge was built, a snake and turtle lived here and caused the waves. On the other side of the stone, four characters say "God (Shangdi, 上帝) sat here." Obliging locals will point out the impression left by Buddha's buttocks when he sat there trying to dissuade the snake and turtle from wreaking such havoc with the tides and waves.

Sichuan or Xichuan   There is a fascinating legend behind the pavilion with "Xichuan" inscribed upon it. During the Ming Dynasty, when Quanzhou was suffering from a prolonged drought, the Mayor of Quanzhou, Fang Ke, asked people to pray for rain.   Evidently, their god wasn't up on geography because he sent an angel to give Sichuan (the west of China) a good wetting down.

As the angel passed through Quanzhou he took pity upon the parched landscape, but he dared not release the

Xi Chuan

rain anywhere but the god's designated target. But Mayor Fang Ke was a savvy politician. He renamed the area Xichuan, evidently figuring that god could not read (because the characters are different even if they sound similar). The angel must have agreed about his lord's literacy, because he released his rain upon Quanzhou (and Sichuan had to make do with bottle water). Hence the stone pavilion's inscription, "Xichuan Ganyu" (西川甘雨), which I was told meant, "Water is precious, one drop is invaluable."

Arm and a Leg A village temple north of the bridge used to be the bridge construction office, and is dedicated to the god who safeguarded its construction. The last Zhuangyuan of the Qing Dynasty, from Jinjiang, wrote the inscription above the temple door.

An arm and a leg...

The temple has a red faced idol of an ancient monk, whom locals revere because, according to legend, when the people lacked fuel for cooking he used his own leg as firewood. "The monk really existed!" I was told, "Though we can't prove the leg story."

Personally, I thought they were just pulling my leg. But I confessed, "American restaurants are worse. They charge an arm **and** a leg."

Getting to Luoyang Bridge: Buses, 10, 13, and 19

Hours: 8:00 — 17:30   **Phone**: 265-1816

Luoyang Cuisine   Speaking of food... Luoyang has some legendary seafood—and it doesn't cost an arm or a leg. Awesome oysters, the size of small eggs; steamed fish soup, washed down by oolong tea that is all the better because of the excellent local spring water; and crabs that are supposedly better than Xiamen's

Heavenly Luoyang Oysters

because they are wild, not cultivated, and served in a thick sauce much like a Western gravy, but redolent of Chinese medicinal herbs. Heavenly.

Luoyang Fish

The Legend of Luoyang Bridge

Neptune's Advice There are many legends about Cai Xiang. One says he tried ten times to lay Luoyang Bridge's foundation, but each time it was swept away by the powerful tides. In frustration, he sent an officer to find the Sea God and ask advice. The officer returned from who knows where with a one word suggestion, "Vinegar." Cai Xiang interpreted this cryptic word, and laid the bridge successfully.

Rev. Pitcher (*In and About Amoy*, 1912) shares one of my favorite accounts:

"It was during one of these squalls that a very remarkable thing happened, which led to the building of the bridge. At this particular time, while a large boat load of passengers was being ferried across, a storm came down upon them in wildest fury. Just when all hope was about to be abandoned of ever reaching the shore a voice rang out above the storm commanding one named Cai（茶）to build a bridge across this dangerous point of the sea. They were soon after all safely landed. It was discovered later that there was but one person by the name of Cai living in that neighborhood. It was also learned that he had only just married, and that it had been revealed to his wife in some mysterious manner that she would be the mother of the man who was to build the bridge.

"In due time the child was born who was named Cai Xiang and grew up a precocious youth. In his young manhood he became a mandarin. His mother took pains to tell him what had occurred in the storm, of what had been revealed to her years before, and what his mission therefore in life might be expected to be. Young Cai became deeply impressed and took steps at once to secure an appointment as mandarin in his native prefecture that he might undertake his appointed task. He knew it was against all custom and law for one to be appointed to office in his own district, he was therefore not a little puzzled to know how this desire of his was to be brought about. But fortune often favors those who are in earnest and in course of time circumstances brought out friend Cai to the palace of the Emperor, where he hit upon a novel as well as bold idea to accomplish his wish.

"One day while walking in the Imperial grounds he took a pot of honey and wrote on a tree this sentence—"Cai Xiang the learned, be magistrate in your native prefectural city." Sometime after the Emperor came walking along, and what his surprise was can only be imagined when he saw this sentence now emblazoned on a tree in living characters of armies of black ants that were feeding on the honey. His surprise found expression as he read out in a loud tone of voice, "Cai Xiang the learned, be magistrate in your native prefectural city." Mr. Cai was conveniently near at hand, and at the same time innocently enough took the words of the Emperor as an appointment to the office he so much desired, and proceeded without delay to thank his sovereign for the great honor he had conferred on him. Though the Emperor protested that that was not at all his meaning—that he was merely reading the sentence which the ants had written (which by the way Cai had taken good pains to bring about, having carefully selected a tree with an ant nest at the base)—he held his majesty to the words as his intention to appoint him to this office. Finally the Emperor yielded...

"He began at once making preparation for building the bridge. His greatest task was in laying the foundations for the central piers as in that particular spot the rushing current never ceases its flow and ebb. How to sink the foundations there puzzled Cai Xiang for many a day, when it occurred to him to write to Neptune on the subject, asking him to be kind enough to keep the waters back from the place for one brief day, and to be so accommodating as to mention the date when that would occur. Then the question arose who was to take this letter to old Neptune.

In answer it was discovered that there was a man living near by whose name was 'Able to Descend into the Sea.' This man was pressed into service and like a bold knight he set out to fulfill his mission, by laying himself down in a comfortable and dry spot where he proposed to stay until the incoming tides covered him, when he could communicate with the god of the waters. While he was waiting he fell asleep. How long he slept will never be known, but when he awoke he found the letter gone, and another addressed to Cai Xiang, though he was in the same spot that he was when he went to sleep.

The letter was delivered to Cai Xiang. It contained but a single character 醋 (vinegar). It was indeed as gall and vinegar to receive such a message, for whatever could it mean! Struggle as he might with it, search his brain hard and long, he could make no sense out of it. Finally he began to break up the character into its different compound parts, and thereby he solved the problem and received his answer from old Neptune. The reply was that at evening on the 21st of the month the waters would be stayed. Thus: 二十一日西. These directions were followed, the foundations successfully sunk and in due time the building of the wonderful bridge completed."

Dongguan Bridge (东关桥) a wooden covered bridge, between Dehua and Putian, is remote, but this provincial level protected relic is a beauty—especially since an Overseas Chinese donated 1 million Yuan to renovate it. Built in 1145 A.D. (15th year of Shaoxing in South Song Dynasty, in case you're dying to know), in Dongmei Village, Dongping Township, this magnificent 85m by 5m wooden beam bridge spans the scenic Humei Brook.

(Photo courtesy Overseas Chinese Museum)

Like other ancient wooden bridges, it has a shrine in the middle, and religious paintings on the beams above. The wooden bridge is supported by stone block columns, with the upstream side shaped like a ship's bow to deflect heavy currents (like Luoyang and Anping bridges).

Getting There: Special bus from Quanzhou to Yongchun
Hours: 8:00 — 17:30   **Phone**: 388-4202

Xiamen Bridge Museum Though in Xiamen, not Quanzhou, this is right next door, and the best way to appreciate China's contributions to bridge building. The museum has models and photos of bridges all over

China, and the rest of the world, as well as the best location to take photos of Xiamen's beautiful Haicang Suspension Bridge. (I'd tell you what world records it has set, but I want to keep you in suspense).

And now... Hui'an maidens and walled cities...

Chapter 7

Hui'an

Walled City, Stonemasons and Hui'an Maidens

"…an out-of-the-way village, in the county of Hui'an, or Gracious Peace. The situation of this village is a most picturesque and beautiful one. Just outside of it, Toa-bu, or the "Great Mother" rises abruptly from the plain, and towers up amidst the peaks and mountain-tops that range themselves around it… In front of it there flows a stream that comes out of the heart of the mountain, its waters pure and sparkling, and as yet undefiled by their touch with the outer world. It never dries up, for its fountains repose deep in the bosom of those everlasting hills; and no summer's drought, nor fiery-faced sun can penetrate to where they lie. Its music, too, never dies out, for jutting rocks, and stones worn smooth, and curves and winding passages, and miniature falls make it sing an endless song." Reverend John Macgowan, "The Story of the Amoy Mission, 1889).[1]

Amoymagic.com

Walled City of Chongwu

Hui'an's many claims to fame include the walled city of Chongwu (the best preserved Ming Dynasty wall in China, and one of only 3 or 4 walled cities left in the country), the uniquely costumed Hui'an maidens (Fujian's most unusual people group), and miles of beautiful beaches unlike any others! Locals said of Chongwu's 13 kilometer beach, "American scientists say the sand is unlike any other sand on earth. Each grain is six-sided, and therefore very healthful for the body!"

Well, I've always thought this was another planet in the first place. But Hui'an's biggest drawing card is not its extraterrestrial sand but its stone, which locals have been carving for 1700 years.

Extraterrestrial Beaches?

Hui'an Stonemasons
Over 120,000 of Hui'an's 920,000 folks work with stone! When Beijing needed stonemasons to build the People's Hall and Tiananmen Square in the 1950s, they shipped in workers from Hui'an, because with over 1700 years of stonemasonry under their belt, they are China's best.

Hui'an stone products –everything from furniture, and tomb stones to carvings of deities, demons, Mickey Mouse, and American presidents—attract tourists and buyers from all over China and Southeast Asia/ (Take a statue home in your carry-on! After courting a hernia you won't take it for granite!).

Getting a head in life

Shadow Carving Hui'an stonemasons may be the best but they aren't resting on their laurels. They continue to develop new materials, products, and techniques, including innovative shadow carving that would have Fred Flintstone clamoring for a family portrait.

Tracing

Shadow carvers reproduce virtually any painting or photograph by tracing it onto a polished slab of marble, tapping out the design, dot by painstaking dot, and coloring it in. The figures are so realistic they look ready to jump off the stone.

Give the artists a good, high resolution family photo

Taps

and they'll copy it for you, and mail it to your home! An 8 x 10 runs from 200 to 300 Yuan, depending upon the level of artistry desired (with some, dots are visible, whereas others really do resemble photos).

Shadow Carving Magic

Get good prices and service at the little green shop just inside the stone gate (with two elephants in front). Mr. Wang Hong also has good prices on jade jewelry, and the little painted resin Hui'an Maiden figurines make nice gifts (small, light, easy to carry or mail) for folks back home.

Flintstone's Studio!

Mr. Wang Hong 汪 洪

Custom shadow carving and Hui'an souvenirs
地址: 惠安县崇武旅游区大门内 (0595)768-6918 768-2190

B.B.

General Lin Lu - Father of Fujian Lins   We know that Hui'an folk have been stone masons for at least 1700 years because the carved granite tomb of General Lin Lu, ancestor of all Fujian Lins, is over 1700 years old. You can visit this "Holy Land of Lins" at Tuling village, north of Hui'an about 20 minutes on

Holy Land of Lin Clan

the 324 highway (by the #144 km marker). There's not really that much historical about the place, since the tomb has been completely made over now with new granite sculptures and concrete. But it's something to think that all of Fujian's Lins descended from this man, who in turn was the descendant of a man hiding out in the woods.

The Story of the Lins
By Miss Qu Weiwei

Bigan (比干) was a famous prime minister during the Shang Dynasty, and uncle of the stupid emperor Zhou (纣). An honest man, Bigan was forever pointing out his stupid nephew's mistakes. Eventually the heartless emperor had had enough, and cut open Bigan's heart (which did him little good because he was still heartless). The furious emperor wanted to kill Bigan's pregnant wife too, but she ran off and hid in a stone house in a forest (林, Lin), where she gave birth to a son whom she named Jian (坚, meaning hard, solid, strong).

Some years later, another tribe toppled the Shang Dynasty and set up the Zhou Dynasty (周朝). The new emperor respected Bigan's honesty, so he found his son Jian and gave him the surname of Lin because the forest had protected him from death.

So Bigan's descendant was General Lin Lu, ancestor of all Fujian Lins, including the great hero Lin Zexu, the famed write Lin Yutang, and the sea goddess Mazu (whose real name was Lin Moliang).

Chongwu (崇武) **Walled City.**   Chongwu is China's best preserved Ming Dynasty Walled city (one of only 3 left, I was told). This delightful town, with its uniquely clad Hui'an Maidens (considered Fujian's most exotic people group) is just up the coast from Quanzhou city and perched upon the horn-shaped Chongwu Peninsula. Originally an

Father to son...

easily defended sentry post prized by famous heroes like Koxinga, the first Ming emperor, Zhu Yuanzhang, changed the name from Dousai to Chongwu, which means "advocating of arms," (maybe the Emperor was a Republican?). The walled city is well worth a visit—and fortunately you no longer have to endure Abortion Road to get there.

Abortion Road   In the early '90s, the road to Chongwu was so bad that locals called it "Abortion Road" because no pregnant lady could take the pot holes and bumps without losing her child. My first trip from Xiamen to Chongwu took 8 hours, and we bounced so hard that I hit my head several times on the bus roof—which was 18 inches above my head! Fortunately, today it is smooth sailing all the way—but a century ago even an 8 hour trip would have seemed miraculous! In the 19th century, Mr. G. Philips wrote that the trip from Fuzhou to Quanzhou,

> "which also takes five days to travel over, is bleak and barren, lying chiefly along the sea-coast, and in winter a most uncomfortable journey..."   (Nowadays, it's only a 2 hour drive!)

Chongwu's 2.4 km wall is easily the best preserved Ming Dynasty wall in existence, and constructed entirely of Hui'an's greatest natural resource: granite. By day and night all throughout Hui' An, young and

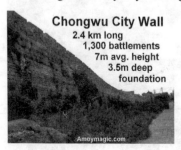
Chongwu City Wall
2.4 km long
1,300 battlements
7m avg. height
3.5m deep
foundation

old alike chip away with stone and chisel to create everything from intricate temple dogs and garden lanterns to Mickey Mouses (or Mickey Mice?). They also build granite homes—and I know for a fact they're cold in the winter! Worse yet, the poor men have no one to snuggle up too, as you're about to learn...

Hui'an Costumes (all blondes?)

Hui'an Maid
Shadow Carving

Hui'an Maidens   (Adapted from *Amoy Magic*).   Chongwu's isolation on its peninsula prevented the ancient Baiyue people from assimilating into the Han culture, so much of their unique culture and dress still survives today.   Considered Fujian's most unique people group (though they are Han Chinese), they lure both tourists and social scientists with their unique fashions and strange marriage customs.

Unique Costumes   Chinese say Hui'an girls have democratic bellies and feudal heads because their tight, short jackets and skintight black hip huggers that flare out baggily at the legs leave their bellies bare, but they fastidiously cover their heads with scarves. A Chongwu girl told me they emphasize the belly because in the Minnan dialect, belly "bazai" sounds like the Mandarin "facai" (to prosper). She also said the blouses were probably short to keep them out of the sea when they bend over the nets.

Amoymagic.com

"Democratic Belly"

Scarves Hui'an women have more scarves than Imelda Marcos has shoes. Miss Huang said they average 120 or so scarves, and some accumulate over 300. "The scarf makes my round face look longer and prettier," she explained. "And older ladies think scarves help them recover their youth."

Derriere Dowry Unmarried Hui'an girls wear a wide, colorfully embroidered belt, but Miss Huang was evidently married because she sported the heavy silver belt (from 1 ½ to 6 ½ pounds!) that is not only a girl's dowry but also her marital insurance. "My husband doesn't dare leave me," she said, "because I have all his wealth around my waist!" (Imagine so much silver going to waist!)

Derriere Dowry

Photo Foes Hui'an women are notorious for hating being photographed. Miss Huang said many of them share a superstition common around the world—that being photographed shortens one's life. One wonders how such a *negative* outlook on photography *develops*.

Tying the Knot I like Hui'an costumes; I even have a small statue of one on my desk in the MBA Center. But I doubt they leave their bellies bare simply to keep the blouses dry. I think the uncovered tummy is simply a tantalizing "revenge" for an ancient insult by a member of the lesser male species.

Legend has it that long ago, a young girl refused to marry a wealthy man. The man was determined to tie the knot, though, so he bound her up, carried her off, and married her in spite of her protests. Even today, the designs around shirts' sleeves and waists are said to remind Hui'an girls of their tragic ancestor's bonds. I also suspect the marriage customs are a form of eternal revenge upon all men.

Not This Year Dear...   Ancient custom forbids bride and groom staying together on their wedding night, so the groom stays in a friend's house. On day two, the bride pays respects to the groom's family and gives gifts to the elders. On day three, the groom's sister leads the bride to the communal well to draw two buckets of water. After five days of obeying various customs, she returns to her parents' home. Bride and groom are not allowed to live together until she bears a child. But here I conceive a problem: when does she conceive?

Don't take these women for granite!

Until a child is born, a woman cannot stay with her husband or even talk to him. If she meets him on the street she must treat him as if he were a stranger. If her husband visits her home, she must wait in back until he leaves.   The newlyweds   are allowed to stay together only 3 times a year: Spring Festival, Grave Sweeping Day, and Mid-Autumn Festival.

Hui'an lassies may be bothersome brides, but they are also indefatigable laborers. They clean house by night and spend all day lugging ponderous loads of rock or grain on baskets slung over their deceptively petite shoulders. Meanwhile, the men fish, or chisel stone in quarries, or hawk victims for their motorcycle taxis, or hang out in tea shops moaning because their bride just told them, "Not this year, dear. I have a headache."

"Not this year, dear.
I have a headache."

Chongwu Religion Religion is a big part of Chongwu life, and with wives like theirs, I can see why. On festivals, Chongwu people light candles and incense and offer sacrifices in the Temple of the 12th Lord, but nowadays, many also attend the newly renovated and expanded Protestant church, which was first built in the 1880s. As late as 1995, members sat on pews made of tree trunks split in half, but now the church has been rebuilt and

A Chongwu Church

expanded, and equipped with genuine pews, much to my derriere's delight. Chongwu's Catholic church attendance has also grown a lot recently. But Chongwu's most unique temple, by far, is dedicated to 27 PLA (People's Liberation Army) soldiers.

PLA Temple Imagine a temple that plays not Buddhist chants but revolutionary songs! Chongwu has one, thanks to Ms. Zhenghen, who grinned and hugged me like I was the prodigal son come home, then

PLA Temple

gave me the red carpet tour of her red army temple, and told me the story behind it.

Zhenghen's family moved from Singapore to Chongwu when she was twelve. The following year, September 17th, 1949, the thirteen year old girl was strolling the beach when Taiwanese bombers began strafing the shore. Gallant

Ms. Zhenghen

PLA soldiers rushed out to her rescue; 24 died in the attempt. Miss Zhenghen showed her thanks and respect by offering sacrifices and incense to the deceased soldiers.

In 1991, with two million Yuan in donations, she built the PLA temple. Initially, the army objected, fearful she was creating another religion, but in the end they saw it as a great opportunity for folks to show respect for the PLA, and over the years not a few army officers

have visited the unique temple.

Behind the altar loaded down with offerings of fruit, incense, crackers, soda cans, mineral water, wine and roasted watermelon seeds are the 27 little hand painted PLA soldiers. (Three other local PLA martyrs were added for good measure). The figurines are fully uniformed

Offerings

and supplied with rifles and pistols, mobile phones, whistles, first aid kits (a bit late for that!) and everything else a soldier needs. The 27 inhabitants are surrounded by toy tanks, airplanes, police cars, battleships, toy mobile phones, and a pink plastic grand piano with a clown at the keyboard.

Well supplied--forever!

Miss Zhenghen has come a long way from the 13-year-old girl paying her respects with incense and fruit. I daresay that in a few centuries, folks will repeat the tale of how the 27 heavenly warriors descended upon a cloud to save Zhenghen from the evil minions across the Dire Straits.

Forest of Statues   I think the Walled City's greatest attraction is... the Walled City! But even though this is the best preserved Ming Dynasty wall in China, many Chinese tourists give it but a cursory glance and head to the seaside to view Chongwu's biggest tourist attraction—the forest of 500 new statues.   Why

Over 500 statues in this stone forest

bother? You can see thousands, for free, in the stores and factories lining former Abortion Highway. But one walk through the Forest of Statues and I changed my tune.

Over 500 statues portray fascinating people and events in history and literature (like "Dream of Red Mansions" 红罗蒙).   The 108 famous generals are also a big hit (Chinese are really into generals; I doubt I could name a dozen American generals if my life depended upon it).

Tales from Dreams of Red Mansions

Foreigners should hire a good guide to explain the stories behind the statues. For example, I'd have never known that the polished black bull was also of stone, and that it gave you good luck if you smacked it.

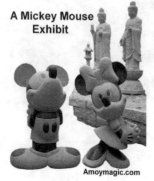
A Mickey Mouse Exhibit

Amoymagic.com

Sounded like a lot of bull to me, but I smacked it, and the stone bull rang like a bell. I especially liked the chubby Maitreya Buddha, which I told my hosts looked like a Disney dwarf. "No way!" he said. "This beats Disney!"   But I must have worried them because when I visited again a few months later, a granite Mickey Mouse stood behind Maitreya—for good measure, perhaps. Pretty mickey mouse, I thought.

Breastfeeding Mom

Filial Piety   A set of 24 statues represent the model sons in 24 tales epitomizing Confucius' ideal of filial piety.   Eight-year-old Wu Meng bared his body so mosquitoes would feast upon him first and spare his aged parents. Wang Xiang was so pious that when his wicked stepmother wanted fish in the winter, he lay upon the ice to melt the river with his body heat. Heaven took pity upon him and gave him the fish. A pious daughter breastfeeds her ailing mom. A pious emperor obeyed doctor's orders and tasted his father's excrement to help diagnose his father's disease. Hindsight helped.

Deng deng (or, better yet, dung dung).

Amoymagic.com

Amoymagic.com

Deng deng, and Dung dung

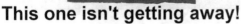

This one isn't getting away!

Black and White Cats My favorite statues are the two colossal cats representing Deng Xiaoping's famous saying, "It does not matter if the cat is black or white as long as it catches rats." The black cat has not only the mouse but also ancient Chinese coins under its paw and on its tail. Noting the lesson here, I thought it appropriate to photograph a famous Hui'an businessman in front (Professor Wu Shinong,vice president—his story is at the end of this chapter).

**Prof. Wu Shinong and Black Cat
Two of a kind!**

Earth Art Many visitors do a double take when they see the boulders strewn along the shore, because some look for the world like a fish, or a turtle. We have a Zhejiang art professor to thank for this "earth art." With a few deft taps of the

Fishy example of "Earth Art"

chisel here and there, he has transformed rocks and boulders into various sea creatures. I was right on top of a giant fish before I saw it. Good thing I wasn't Jonah.

Hot Bread for Taiwan Many of the white ships anchored offshore are from Taiwan! Closer to Taizhong harbor (94 miles) than Xiamen, Chongwu was the mainland's first harbor to accept Taiwan ships. Chongwu and Taiwan folk jest that fresh baked Chongwu bread is still hot after making the two hour crossing to Taiwan. With so many delays implementing the long-awaited "San Tong" (Three Links), its nice to see that Chongwu already has her own "Mini San Tong" (小三通).

Amazing Walled City Maze

The walled city is amazing. It's also quite a maze, and easy to get lost. Of course, it's no problem getting out because all you have to do is head in one direction long enough until you reach the wall, which you can ascend to get your bearings before you descend and lose them again. I've considered tying a piece of string

Amazing Maze (everything but maize)

around my waist and reeling myself in afterwards, but some enterprising Hui'an peasant would probably cut the string and sell it. But after much trial and error (mostly error), I've figured out a surefire way of getting in and out.

The walled city has several large gates, and a few small ones. Enter the gate at the top of the narrow road that begins at the Protestant church—and step back in time 300 years! (Except for the kamikaze motorcyclists who career around corners, hands glued

Enter here, exit...where?

to their horns). Just down the path on the left is the Chen family's ancestral home.

Chen's Ancestral Home

Chen Family Ancestral Home

The first time I peeked through the courtyard door of the Chen home, a granny grinned, spouted off something in the dialect, grabbed my arm, and led me inside for tea. They gave me a tour of their home, and showed me the ancestral paintings and photos. They've been in this home for hundreds of years, and much hasn't changed—but Mrs. Chen *does* have a topnotch kitchen. Of course, this came as no surprise. Chinese are not only the planet's best cooks but also the best eaters, spending much of their waking lives cooking and eating delightful (most of the time) foods.

Their son was bent over a giant basin of dough making some of Chongwu's famous fish rolls. This family has sold them for several generations, and I bought about ten pounds to give to friends back home. Sliced and fried, they are heavenly.

"What's cooking, Granny Chen?"

Chen family's fine fish rolls!

At the T My landmark is the "T" intersection's temple (Sue misses it, every time). Turn right at the "T" and

follow South Gate Street (Nanmen Lu 南门路) all the way to the seaside gate.

Note the architecture—the rounded Minnan roofs, and the "flying sparrow" eaves. Also note the tailor, Mr. Chen. He uses a 100 year old Min River sewing machine—much the same as those used a century ago. Newly minted machines are made much the same, but no point in reinventing the wheel. They work, and they don't require electricity.

Ascend the wall opposite the temple and walk north to the lighthouse, which offers a nice view of the walled city, and of the large crescent of a beach, with its fine white extraterrestrial sand (Hui'an has miles of beautiful beaches). Then either return the way you came, or walk along the top of the wall (which helps you avoid the funerals).

See no evil, hear no evil, do no evil

Along the wall to the lighthouse

It seems that every time we visit Chongwu we encounter a long funeral procession of paid professional mourners, musicians – and plastic babies? The tail end of the procession often has several men bearing a litter containing naked plastic baby dolls. I asked what they symbolized but they said they didn't know. Rebirth, perhaps?

After seeing the third funeral in one day, I told an MBA student who was with me, "China has more dying people than any place on the planet."

"That's not true!" he protested. "We have great medical care here."

"It's mathematics, not medicine," I said. "Biggest population, remember?" His feathers slowly unruffled.

Funeral Babies

The Mourning After

The walled city's streets are so narrow there is no way to escape funeral processions, so you just press your back to the wall and cover your ears to shut out the cacophony of cymbals, drums, trumpets, and suona. Suona is the horn commonly played at funerals, but I'd think the shrill device would be more likely to wake the dead than comfort them.

The professional mourners were so surprised to see us Laowai, backs to the wall, that they forgot to wail and stared as us as if we were demons from hell itself, instead of just standard issue foreign devils from afar.   I waved, they grinned and waved back—and then got down to business again, wailing piteously as if in apology to the extinguished object of this parade.

THE STARE

Sue stops, crowd gathers in seconds

3 Minutes Later

7 minutes later, Sue vanishes. Ann abandons her to her fate

The Chinese Stare   One thing that has changed little over the past century is the Chinese Stare.   Everywhere, people gather around the Laowai and stare.   It's unsettling at times, but understandable if you realize that we also stare at unusual sites, or people. If I recognize a movie star in Los Angeles, I do a double take. If I see an

Arab in robes and headdress, I stare. And let's face it—as we Laowai tourists roam the narrow winding streets of Chongwu, we stare at them! Worse, we take photos as they go about their lives, as if they were exhibits.   So if we, the very unusual foreigner, are stared at, or surrounded by crowds, or have parents with little children point at us and say, "See, Little Plum Blossom, that's a foreigner!" (to which I often respond, "I can't help it!"), it's understandable.   But fortunately, the crowds are friendly—and were even back in 1889.

When McGowan wrote *The Story of the Amoy Mission* in 1889, the Chinese were still smarting from the humiliation of defeat in two Opium Wars, and foreigners were not always the most welcome sight. Yet even then, Mcgowan wrote that, once Chinese got to know you,

> "The crowd becomes sympathetic. The sneer dies out of their faces. There is nothing that touches the Chinese heart so mightily as practical benevolence. It is a virtue they highly appreciate. Their stolid, emotionless features begin to light up with genuine feeling, and the eyes of some are twinkling and flashing as their hearts are moved…[what] has just happened has been a mighty revelation. It has brought you closer to the Chinese heart than you were before, and it has revealed to you the wondrous possibilities of the future…"

So as you stare at the places and peoples, accept their good natured stares in return! And given that they *are* going to stare, give them their money's worth, as I do when I talk to the village pigs, goats, chickens, and turkeys (both two and four legged varieties).

Talking Turkey

Huiquan Beer (福建
惠泉啤酒集团股份有
限公司)

Quanzhou is famed
not only for Anxi tea
but also, more recently,
Huiquan Beer. Though
I'm not one to root for
beer (root beer is more
my speed), bona fide
beer aficionados claim
Huiquan beer is one of
China's best—and *the*
best with seafood.

Huiquan Beers

Huiquan has invested hundreds of millions to give Qingdao Beer
(produced in the former German colony) and the imports a good run for
their money.   After Professor Wu Shinong showed me around the
sprawling, modern Huiquan factory, we visited the biergarten downtown
(just outside the old factory), where my companions tasted various brews
while I stared at the sculpture on the back
wall that looked suspiciously a giant
marijuana leaf.

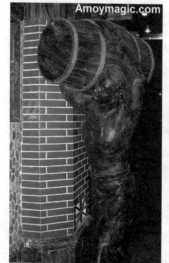

Huiquan Beergarden

Prof. Wu inspects the beer!

I can't really judge Huiquan beer, so I checked with the pros at **www.beeradvocate.com** and found this review by "Stoutman":

"A Chinese surprise!!!! Very light and easy to drink with a hint of fruitiness in the aroma. The yeast culture provides the perfect refreshing spicy and fruity character that is expected of a wheat beer. Even stranger, this beer has an almost pale green color. It also has considerable more hop flavor than any of the traditional wheat styles of beer I have sampled. I generally dislike wheat beers, but this one is good."

Address: #157 Jianshe Street, Huian, Luocheng Township, 362100, PRC
地址：福建惠安螺城建设大街 157 号， 邮编：362100 中国
Phone: 0595 738-2369
Chinese website: **http://www.huiquan-beer.com/index.shtml**

With G.M. Lu and son

Wood Carving   While Hui'an's biggest drawing card is stone carving, the city also has quite a few factories producing quality wood statues. I waltzed in unannounced at the Hui'an Jusheng Crafts Company , and even though they knew I wasn't going to buy, the general manager, Mr. Lu Peiyang (卢培养) and his 16-year-old son Lu Dongqiang (卢东强) , served up the tea and gave me a tour of the four story factory.

Mr. Lu said most of Hui'an's wooden statues are religious objects for export (and suggested I look for secular carvings in Putian or Xianyou, up the coast towards Fuzhou). I was surprised that, given the high quality of the wood and the artistry, the

"Repaint, and thin no more!"

statues were painted, gilded and smothered in wigs and costumes. I asked what the point was of using expensive wood when mass produced plastic or ceramic would look the same. "Tradition," manager Lu said. "Temples want wood."

Jusheng Crafts Address: west side of 324 highway, just north of Luoyang Bridge. Ph: (0595)733-1199 E-mail: lupeiyang@21cn.net

> The spray-painted wooden idols reminded me of the rural Chinese who painted their entire wooden church with only one can of paint, reasoning that if Elijah's oil never ran out, why should their paint? So they prayed and painted, and as the can got low, they added a little thinner, and a little more, until by the end of the job it was mostly thinner—but it worked! And just as they rested from their labors, a mighty downpour washed the thinned paint right off the church, and a voice from heaven commanded, "Repaint, and thin no more!"

Idol Talk   The endless array of wooden idols brought to mind the old Chinese saying, "He who carves the Buddha does not worship them." And I wondered what kind of deities they were, and who on earth (or China) worshipped them. For example, the nattily attired idol wearing a fez and clasping a pile of

gold coins in his lap looked Muslim—which wasn't too farfetched. Muslim traders, after all, were the best businessmen in the ancient Orient.

Malaysia's Nadu Gong
a down-to-earth fellow

But Muslims don't worship idols, and Miss Qu Weiwei checked it out and found he is Nadu Gong (拿督公), a local earth god (土地公, Tudi Gong) for overseas Chinese in Malaysia. When they first moved to Malaysia they discovered the natives worshipped the local earth in the hopes of a good harvest. The Chinese adapted the idea by piling some gold in the down-to-earth deity's lap so he would know just what kind of harvest the enterprising Chinese wanted.

Hui'an artisans bring both wood and stone to life!

Amoymagic.com

Laozi lectures

Haves, and have knots

East Meets West!

For your edification, Overseas Chinese University's Miss Qu Weiwei gives us the stories behind three of the most common idols.

Jigong Living Buddha (济公活佛, or Geekung), a very popular deity for sculptures and paintings, is one of China's most colorful characters. Also called Jidian Monk (济颠), or "Crazy Monk, this wine swilling meat munching monk was loved by the common people because he cared for the poor and put the rich in their place—kind of like a Chinese Robin Hood (罗宾汉) or Zorro.

Jigong was born to the Li family during the South Song Dynasty in Zhejiang province. By age 12, he was already a Xiucai (秀才 skilled writer), but he was obsessed with the sutras and

Jigong, the Mad Monk

became a monk, changing his name from Li Xiuyuan (李修远) to "Daoji" (道济). His unorthodox behavior (he loved meat, especially dog meat, and getting drunk, and acting, in general, like a mad man), earned him the nickname Crazy Monk. Today, a cave by Linyin Temple's (灵隐寺) Flying Stone (飞来峰) has beds and tables named after Jigong because it is said that he went there to roast dogs and guzzle wine.

Jigong used a ratty old folding fan for a weapon, which in his magical hands was deadlier than the sharpest sword. Armed with this magical fan, he fought injustice and punished stupid or bad officials. The Chinese saying for his behavior is, "When encountering injustice, aid the oppressed" (路见不平拔刀相助, lu jian bu ping ba dao xiang zhu). Like Zorro, Jigong fought injustice with style, usually causing the villain to look ridiculous, which earned him the affection of the downtrodden.

Ji Gong prepares to wok his dog

A Jigong biography (《济公传》) was written about the mad monk, and some people believe he was one of the 500 arhats, but because Buddah did not approve of his behavior (especially his wine guzzling and devouring roast dog legs), his statue is always in the temple aisles and not with the other more holy arhats (who still manage some mighty bellies for being vegetarians; I suspect they had a few hot dogs too).

Touching up Nazha, Boy Wonder

Nezha (哪咤), the fat little boy with the funny haircut, is another frequent subject of paintings, sculptures, and folk tales. The story actually come from India. The boy Nalakuvara was said to be the third son of General Li Jing (李靖) in heaven. His father disliked the boy and treated him like a monster because he was in his mother's womb for three years and emerged round like a ball.

Nezha's powerful teacher gave him a magic ring (乾坤圈)—a great gift, but one that led him to his doom when he practiced with it upon the seashore. The ring was so powerful that it stirred up the dragon king's underwater home. Nezha wasn't really trying to make waves, but the infuriated lizard sent his son to fight Nezha. After Nezha killed the dragon's son, the dragon king determined to kill the entire family of General Li Jing (who was much lower rank than the dragon). To save his family, Nezha committed suicide by cutting his body and bones to pieces. His powerful teacher then saved him by using a lotus for his body—thus the origin of the original flower child. Over the years, the legends multiplied. In *Journey to the West* (《西游记》) Nezha even battled the monkey king (but was defeated by the superior simian).

Black and White Wuchangs These two demons stick out above the crowd because their long red tongues are always sticking out, lolling down past their fat chins. Mr. White Wuchang has a white face, white clothes, and a tall white hat upon which are the four characters Tianxia Taiping (天下太平), meaning "All under heaven is peaceful. Mr. Black Wuchang has a black face, black clothes, and a black hat with the characters Yijian Facai (一见发财), meaning, "You prosper as soon as you see him." Both phrases are nice (peace, and prosperity), but Chinese fear seeing them because what is the point of either peace or prosperity if you're dead?

Mr. White and Mr. Black have different personalities but the same job

White Wuchang

Amoymagic.com

Dynamic Duo
(a little tongue in cheek there!)

description: kill folks and escort their souls to hell, where they are judged by the king of hell after they have undergone various procedures and ordeals such as crossing the Naihe bridge (奈何桥), where they must drink the Mengpo Soup (孟婆汤) so that they forget everything that happened during their life.

It seems a bit unfair to be judged for a life you've totally forgotten, but Mengpo soup or not, in Chinese mythology, once you die there is hell to pay.

Supplement

Professor Wu Shinong
—a Hui'an Entrepreneur

It's easier to understand Hui'an's rapid economic growth when you've spent a few years in the shadow of a Hui'an entrepreneur like Professor Wu Shinong, of Xiamen University's MBA Center. He epitomizes the local talent and drive that made ancient Zaytun a City of Light, and that is rekindling that light today.

Prof. Wu Shinong

Wu Shinong was born in Hui'An county, and after graduating from high school in 1974, he spent four years as a factory worker during the Cultural Revolution. His parents owned a small grocery store before 1949, and after Liberation escaped being labeled capitalists because of their store's small scale—but since then the Wu family have proven to be entrepreneurs to the bone.

After 1949, they became sales people in a State store. Today, they have two houses and several stores. Wu Shinong has three older sisters and one older brother. The brother runs a small watch store, the older sister is retired, the middle sister runs a small transportation company with three trucks, and the youngest sister works at Huiquan Beer (her policeman husband was my guide on one of my Chongwu trips).

Wu Shinong, like the rest of his family, is an entrepreneur. In fact, I joke that his name should be Wu Shibuneng (无事不能) because I suspect there's not much he can't do when he puts his mind to it. But fortunately for me, he has focused his talents on China's future: MBA business education.

In 1978, Wu Shinong entered Xiamen University, majoring in economics, and in '86 received an MBA from Dalhousie in Canada. From 1987 he worked on a joint Ph.d. program between Xiamen University and Dalhousie; spending two years in Xiamen and one year in Dalhousie, was a Fulbright scholar in Stanford in 1994, and returned to Xiamen in 1995. Today, he is one of the three vice chairmen of China's MBA Education Supervision Commission.

Though young (my age!), Professor Wu Shinong has been integrally involved in every step of China's development of management education, beginning with the initial feasibility study in 1987 to 1989, and the test group for MBA education in China (18 professors from 9 universities organized this).

In 1999, Prof. Wu was selected as one of the ten Chinese professors who have had the most influence on empirical research in economics and management. The prolific professor has written 4 books on his own, co-authored three, and published 60 pieces in leading journals. He also helped translate Steven Ross' bestseller, "Corporate Finance." Prof. Wu was the first person in China to study security market efficiency, and the effect of financial information on capital markets.

Early on, Prof. Wu upset the apple cart when he published a paper on China's accounting in *General Accounting Research*. In part because Professor Wu is not an accountant, traditional economists heatedly argued his points, but younger scholars recognized the validity of his arguments and approach. During his studies, Professor Wu saw that the holistic viewpoint was crucial—"seeing the interrelationships between capital markets, accounting information, and how they affect one another and investors."

Professor Wu, who studied economics and statistics, said,

"In 1991, because the Chinese capital market was just established, there was no precedence, very short history, and no promotion of empirical studies. In 1995 I started thinking about this problem, and we had a better information base at that time, and I was able to show that the capital market did react to financial information, and corporations' announcements. So I started thinking about this. In 1993 I wrote the first paper about capital market efficiency, but I only had 16 firms from Shanghai and Shenzhen security exchange to study. It was a small number, but it was only the first attempt. Nowadays we have larger samples— sometimes more than 1000 firms. And now you can find that there is relatively stable behavior, or patterns to examine, and you can compare or use western capital market theory to apply to China's situation, and you can see differences, and explore the reasons for the differences. There are so many questions of interest."

Regarding Xiamen University MBA, Professor Wu said,

"Only a handful of Universities can offer comprehensive Ph.D.s in management (in all specialties). Xiada is one of them. In July 1990, Xiada was the first Chinese university allowed to offer a Chinese MBA; Nankai followed one week later. MBA degrees weren't official then, so the graduation certificates said, "Economics (Business Administration M.A.)." Students were upset, so we called it the "Masters of Economics (Business Administration).

"Nankai, like Xiada, began as a joint project with Canada. They had the first graduates one week after Xiamen University MBA— they were told by Beijing to follow the procedures already worked out with Xiamen University."

In his copious free time, Professor Wu is a husband and father--and judging from his daughter, doing pretty well at that too. His daughter is a math wiz, excels at English and Chinese is in the top 15 of her school, and wants to study journalism, law, or management—first at Beijing University, and then at Harvard, Stanford, or Cambridge.

Notes

[1] Macgowan, Rev. John, "The Story of the Amoy Mission," reprinted by Ch'eng Wen Publishing Company, Taipei, 1971. Originally by Butler & Tanner, The Selwood Printing Works, Frome, and London, August, 1889, p.127)

Chapter 8

Nan An
— Home of Koxinga

Koxinga

Jiuri Mountain (九日山)   The official starting point of the Silk Road of the Sea was not Quanzhou city proper but Jiuri (9th Day) Mtn in Nan'An, about 7 km from Quanzhou City's west gate.   The Han Chinese had a big (or actually, a very small) reason for not settling down on the coast—mosqui toes.

"Jiuri Mountain"

The coast teemed with malarial mosquitoes, and tens of thousands died. Only after a massive land reclamation effort, which drained the malarial marshes, were Chinese able to move to the coast itself.   But Jiuri was an auspicious place to begin because of its perfect "fengshui" ("wind and water" – the Chinese geomancy that dictates much of Chinese life).

A Chinese guide in N.E. Fujian told me that a NASA photo showed glowing spots all over China, and on inspection they all turned out to be ancient tombs—thus proving, scientifically, the validity of fengshui (either that, or China has a few dozen Chernobyls).

The mountain is called Jiuri (9th day) because from the Jin to the Song Dynasties, dispossessed nobles in Quanzhou climbed the mountain each year on the ninth day of the ninth month, and gazed with longing towards their former home in the north. And here they performed the Safe Passage Ceremony, for both Chinese and foreign ships, to the "God of Transportation" (precursor of California Highway Maintenance).

Yanfu Temple. Fujian's oldest temple (or second oldest, some argue), was built in 288 A.D. at the base of Jiuri Mountain, facing the river to the south, with hills on the west, east and north, like an armchair. Jiuri offers ideal "fengshui"—and a picturesque pallet for centuries of calligraphers.

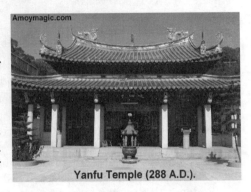

Yanfu Temple (288 A.D.).

At Dr. Lim's we met a calligrapher of note. Persuaded to write an inscription for us, his brush almost miraculously brought life and movement to the paper. With a superbly graceful precision, his hand seemed to be evoking beauty that was already there, rather than making a dogmatic statement. But the Chinese have, it seems, always known that truth and beauty cannot be taken by storm.
Averil Mackenzie-Grieve[1]

Chinese Scholar (Smith, 1908)

Calligraphy   While Yanfu Temple is one of Jiuri Mountain's 36 official sites, the real drawing card is calligraphy. My Chinese guide boasted, "Every meter of these cliffs is covered in ancient   calligraphy!" Rather   like   American subways, I thought.

Jiuri Mtn. Calligraphy

UNESCO Calligraphy   Jiuri even has English calligraphy!   The 1991 UNESCO Maritime Silk Road Expedition visited Jiuri Mountain and left an English inscription, with signatures in many Western languages.   The English UNESCO inscription reads,

"Seven centuries after the 'begging wind' inscription a new inscription illustrating friendship and dialogue will be added to Jiuri   Hill.   We,   the international team of the UNESCO maritime route expedition,   who   have traveled from Africa, the Americas,   Asia,   and Europe   on   board   the "Fulk al Falan" ship of Hefoe   lent   for   the occasion by the Sultan of Oman,   are   here   as pilgrims   not   only   to renew that age old prayer but   also   to   carry   the message   of   peace between peoples which is the ultimate aim of the UNESCO integral study of the silk road. Roads of dialogue.   15th February 1991, International Team Maritime Route Expedition."

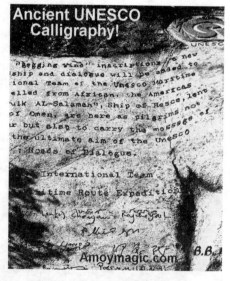

Ancient UNESCO Calligraphy!

The most important inscriptions are the records of the sacrificial rites held by South Song Dynasty Quanzhou officials when they prayed for smooth sailing (what UNESCO called "begging winds", I suppose). Other key inscriptions include those by famous philosopher Zhu Xi, and the unique inscription by Luoyang Bridge's builder Cai Xiang. Where other calligraphers wrote on paper and had it transferred to stone, Cai Xiang wrote directly on the stone—but what would one expect from a man who could get bridge building advice from King Neptune himself?

Chenxu Pavilion

Near the peak, a concrete pavilion (crafted to resemble wood) honors the esteemed poet Chenxu, who lived there 23 years. A round, flat stone is inscribed with 翻经石 (Translating Sutras Stone), in memory of the Indian monk (拘那罗陀, Indian name, or 真谛三藏, Chinese name), who lived here about 300 A.D. while translating Buddhist scriptures into Chinese. He must have had company because he scratched a Chinese chess board into a stone.

One of the most unusual inhabitants was a monk who lived in a tiny cave for 44 years. Some say he was Chinese, others say Indian. Regardless, its hard to believe he could have spent his entire life in that hole-in-the-wall.

40 Years Here!

Stone Buddha (石佛) is 300 years older than the Old Stone Saint in Quanzhou. After he lost his head during the Cultural Revolution, Hui'an artisans crafted a cement head, which probably helps give Stone Buddha a more concrete philosophy on life. Whatever the case, this is certainly one Buddha who won't take getting ahead for granite.

Getting to Jiuri: Bus: # 6, or special tourist bus line # 602

Hours: 8:00 — 17:30

This Stone Buddha offers concrete advice

Mr. Cai

Minnan Village Cultural Landmark (蔡资深古民居) For a delightful look at 19th century life, visit Nan'an's sprawling Minnan village just south of Guanqiao, and 2 km west of the 324 highway. The 16 house complex, which now has 200 residents, was built between 1865 and 1911 by Mr. Cai Qian （Cai Zeshen), a Nan An native with three brothers and ten sons. At age 16 he emigrated to the Philippines,

Mr. Cai's Minnan Village

where he prospered, and after carving a name for himself in the Philippine history books, he returned to Nan An to carve (literally) a home for himself and his descendants.

None Like Mr. Cai's   What makes Mr. Cai's home really stand out is the profusion of intricate stone, wood and tile carvings, from granite foundations to intricate ceramic eaves. The endless carvings gave rise to a local saying, "You can have millions, but not have a house like Mr. Cai."

Mr. Cai serves tea

The caretaker, a 4th generation descendant of Mr. Cai, gave us tea, and then a tour. The village has stone sidewalks covering the drainage, firewalls between each row of buildings, and large courtyards to dry grain.   As I entered the home, I was told that Minnan homes always had 3 steps to represent Tian (天,heaven), Di (地, earth), and Ren (仁, benovelence). There are also four doors, and a Minnan tradition reminds one to "respect parents when entering the right door," and "respect others like brothers" when exiting the left door. Of course, one should never, ever, enter through the two center doors!

Doors   Traditional houses had four front doors, but the two center doors, with their brightly painted celestial guardians, were always kept barred, and opened only for the Emperor.   Everyone else, including the master of the house (and her husband) used the side doors.

Last year, a man in West Fujian threw open his center doors with a flourish and said, "Only for the emperor—and today, for you!" It was a nice gesture, but with everyone watching, I could not bring myself to step over the lintel, so I said, "Not even us American devils are that fat!" And as my host laughed, I slipped in through the right door.

"No house like Cai's"

Tile Carvings

Filial son with fishy motives thaws river

Ming Dynasty Styrofoam The chipped corner of an old, richly carved "beauties bench" (美人,靠, upon which footbound beauties spent their days on display) revealed not wood but some white material. I looked closer and discovered it was Styrofoam! But I wasn't overly surprised. Chinese invented everything else, so why not

Ancient styrofoam?

Styrofoam? But it turned out that a 20 part TV series about Koxinga's descendants had been filmed here and this was just a leftover prop.

Well done!

Mr. Cai's Unusual Well Chinese love wells, the older the better—like the 1,000 year-old-well at Ashab Mosque, or the 2,000-year-old well at Wuyi Mountain's Minyue King Palace. And of course, they swear that the water in each well is as clear as the day it was dug (regardless of decades of tourists losing within its depths their eyeglasses, cameras, handkerchiefs). Mr. Cai's well was not old, but it was allegedly very unusual. The water is supposedly warm in winter and cool in summer. Professor Wu Shinong drew some water from the well to prove the point, but it seemed neither hot nor cold to me so I spew it out. Near the well was the Cai clan stone tub in which girls bathed in water to which had been added aromatic herbs.

Virgin Mazu? The ancestral shelf's various gods included a local god with a flowing white beard, and a small Pusa that evoked quite a debate. One man claimed it was the Virgin Mary, because Mr. Cai had spend most of his life in the predominately Catholic Philippines. Another argued she was a Buddhist goddess, perhaps Guanyin

Virgin Mazu?

(the Hindu god who had a sex change to become the Chinese goddess of mercy). Yet another said it was Mazu, who like Mary was also a virgin, and therefore perhaps the same person. I stayed out of the conversation.

Eclectic Architecture
Given the architecture, who knows what religion they worshipped! One wall's base has a Hindu lotus motif, while a nearby roof has Muslim style eaves (the roof dragons, by the way, were allowed on the homes of 7th level government officials or higher).

7th level or higher

Tom ate Jerry?

Tom & Jerry Many carvings illustrate historical stories or fables. One wall's base has a granite mouse stealing a gourd, but his days are numbered because a granite cat is eyeing him. A wooden wall carving depicts the 24 models of Confucian filial piety that we saw represented in Chongwu's Field of Statues—the son baring his arm for mosquitoes to keep them off his parents, the youth melting ice with his bare back to get a fish for his ailing wicked stepmother, the maid breastfeeding her ailing mother, the pious Emperor tasting his father's excrement to help diagnose his disease, deng deng and dung dung. We could also learn a lesson or two from the headless horseman…

Headless Horseman
During the Cultural
Revolution, Red Guards
destroyed cultural treasures
in even the most remote
places, so Mr. Cai's home,
so close to a highway, was
not neglected. They
destroyed or defaced

Headless horseman

carvings, and chiseled off so many heads and faces that Mr. Cai's house
has more headless horsemen than Sleepy Hollow. Like the carvings of
Confucius' tales, these headless statues also teach us a lesson. (I'm not
sure what it is, but there's bound to be one!).

Elegant old furniture. Rooms were rather bare by
American standards, but what little furniture they
possessed was exquisite. One room was empty except
for a round mahogany table with inlaid marble top, and
benches. The canopied beds now fetch thousands of
dollars in antique stores (though you can get excellent
reproductions at the Arts and Crafts town in Xianyou^2).
Imagine my horror when an Anxi peasant friend told
me they had just burned a beautiful 200-year-old
carved canopy bed because a grandmother had died in
it!

Renovations Endless carvings and calligraphy are nice, but for me it was a bit overkill. What I most appreciated was the sheer functionality of the place, right down to small details like the sliding slatted wooden windows. But if Mr. Cai's mansion cost a pretty penny to build, it is now costing the government a small fortunate to keep it up as well. Nan An's Mayor Chen said the government has spent over one million Yuan in restoration and installation of

Sliding windows

fire alarms, and hires security guards to protect their investment. Unfortunately, these guards are about 30 years too late to stop the Red Guards' from beheading horsemen.

Music to my Ears At the Cai mansion guard gate we came across elderly gents playing traditional instruments. They gave us a rousing performance of Southern Music and Mayor Chen unabashedly belted out the accompaniment for some ancient Minnan folk songs. But high pitched folks songs in the nasally Minnan dialect aren't exactly my cup of tea (or coffee either), and it must have showed. The man playing the

two-stringed Chinese fiddle (二 胡 , erhu) apologetically explained that Minnan singers are limited because they have only the five notes of the ancient pentatonic scale. It sounded to me like they had dozens of notes, and none in a key that I'd ever heard of. But I smiled, and said, "No problem. I know all eight notes and I can't sing either."

Mayor of Nan 'An Enjoys Local Music

Getting There: Bus #9
Hours: 8:00 — 5:30   **Phone:** 6892290

Nan'an Cuisine   After visiting the Cai Mansion, we had a delightful lunch of Nan'an Cuisine (Minnan cuisine, but with some delightful twists I'd not seen elsewhere). I especially enjoyed the lamb rib (羊排, yangpai) with peanut sauce, the taro and black mushrooms, and the Minnan rice with dried oysters and taro (芋头饭). I thought it would be hard to stomach the local specialty, "Twice boiled fish stomach in pork broth" (鱼鳔宝), but it was actually quite tasty. We also enjoyed bitter melon and pine nuts (苦瓜和松子) and Nan'an's most expensive fish, Eastern star fish (东星鱼), which costs 175 Yuan a jin (1.1 lbs) even here in the outback. I think they misnamed it. It should be named Easter 5-star fish! After a dish of hot succulent crab (which Chinese call a "cool" food), we were served piquant ginger tea, which is "hot." This balanced the body's

Nan'an Specialties!

Twice-boiled Fish Stomach

Eastern Star Fish!

Lamb Ribs 'n Peanut Sauce

and other stuff!

"heat" and also cleared the palate for the next course.

As we ate, Mayor Chen explained that the son-in-law of Tan Kah Kee (Chen Jiagen) was born in Nan An, and after the Japanese war most of Xiamen University's money came from the son-in-law, not Tan Kah Kee—hence Xiamen University and Nan An's close relationship. But Nan'an's favorite son is, of course, the Japanese/Chinese pirate-cum-hero liberator of Taiwan, Koxinga! So we trudged off to his ancestral home's Koxinga memorial hall.

Koxinga

Koxinga Memorial Hall （郑成功纪念馆, Zheng Chenggong Jinian Guan). Koxinga, who liberated Taiwan from the Dutch, is as much a hero to the Japanese as the Chinese. For one thing, Koxinga was party "made in Japan"—born in Japan of a Japanese mother and Chinese father from Nan'an. Japanese also admire his bravery and loyalty, and during the 19th century, plays about Koxinga were as popular in Japan as Shakespearean plays in England. Koxinga died in Taiwan and was buried in Tainan until his grandson brought his body back to his ancestral home in 1699, but today Taiwan has over 100 temples dedicated to Koxinga.

Man of Steles The Koxinga memorial has photographs, paintings and artifacts, and to the right of the memorial is a "stele forest" with a large collection of stone steles graced with the calligraphy of famous folks. When I asked how they got important personages to laboriously

Koxinga
Forest of steles

carve out Chinese characters onto stone, my guide looked at me as if I were from outer space and not just another country, and said, "They didn't carve the stone. They wrote it on paper, and workers traced it onto polished granite or marble and carved it out."

I had no idea what they said, but I appreciated their innovativeness. In fact, they were so innovative that my Chinese friends could not read some of them either. (Maybe they were doctor's prescriptions?).

On one stele, all of the characters formed roses. On another, the artists used the beautiful ancient characters that actually resembled what they portrayed (like sun, moon, and mountains) before centuries of scholars so stylized them that they became unrecognizable. One calligrapher drew his characters in such a way that they resembled a scholar (for the life of me I could not figure out what it said).

Calligraphy or charicature?

The exhibit also has some of Koxinga's calligraphy, in which he warned, "Study is most important." Maybe so, but good marksmanship didn't hurt either—especially after the scholar Koxinga burned his Confucian robes and went to war. While Edward Bulwer-Lytton claimed "The pen is mightier than the sword[3]," I suspect the only time that holds true is when the pen is 22 caliber.

After the memorial and forest of steles, check out Koxinga's ancestral

Koxinga's Ancestral Home

home at the bottom of the hill, and then visit the Koxinga Mausoleum.

> **Getting There**: Special Quanzhou Bus to Shuitou (水头)
> **Hours**: 8:00 — 17:30 **Phone**: 698-7138

Koxinga Mausoleum(郑成功陵墓, Zheng Chenggong Lingmu)

> **Getting There**: Special Quanzhou Bus to Shuitou (水头)
> **Hours**: 8:00 — 17:30 **Phone**: 690-8271

The Legend of Koxinga, Pirate-Cum-Patriot

Zheng Chenggong (1624-1662), called Koxinga by the Dutch, was a pirate-cum-patriot who learned his trade from his father Zheng Zhilong. Zheng Zhilong was from Shijing (石井, stone well), at the mouth of Anhai creek (location of the famous Anping Bridge). In his youth he studied foreign trade in Macao, then sailed to Japan and applied Portuguese trade principals to piracy. By the 1620s, Zhilong's enormous fleet literally ruled the Fujian coast. In 1626 and 1627 he attacked and took possession of Amoy (Xiamen) Island, which became the base for his piracy and smuggling operations. In 1628, Zhilong surrendered to the Ming authorities so he could enjoy official status, and as a reward he was promoted to major and then provincial military governor, thus making the transition from pirate to politician (which was not much of a transition). By now, Zhilong's family were practically the overlords of Fujian province, and with his tremendous wealth, he built a walled town south of Quanzhou in Anping (Anhai), which became a prosperous trading center.

Zheng Zhilong supplemented his enormous fortune by selling protection to traders—which they dared not refuse, because Zhilong had over 1,000 ships and a private navy under his control. But Zheng Zhilong sealed his fate when he surrendered to the Manchus after they invaded Fujian, because he was opposed by no less than his son, Koxinga.

Somewhere in Zhilong's busy pirating schedule he had found time to marry a Japanese maid, Miss Tagawa, who bore a son: Fu Song, aka Zheng Chenggong, aka Koxinga. Legends claim that stars fell and the heavens sang on the night of his birth.

When Koxinga was seven, his father shipped him back to the ancestral home of Nan An for schooling. Zheng Zhilong, like all fathers before and since, wanted his son to have what he did not have as a youth—namely, lots of homework.

Koxinga was an excellent scholar and survived both school and homework, and at age 21 headed off to Nanjing State College, never dreaming that his future lay not in scholastics but in piracy and politics—thanks to the militant Manchus.

After a peasant army overthrew the Ming dynasty, the Manchus waltzed into the power vacuum and created the Qing Dynasty. After a fight in Fuzhou in 1646, Tagawa (Koxinga's mother) was raped by Manchus on Amoy and she committed suicide. When Koxinga's father surrendered, Confucian filial piety dictated that Koxinga also throw in the towel (remember the 24 parables of Confucian piety?), but for some reason (perhaps his mother's suicide?), Koxinga parted ways with his father and in 1647, at the tender age of 23, with 90 something followers he began his Gulangyu-islet based anti-Ming rebellion.

Koxinga changed Xiamen's name to Siming (思明, "Remember the Ming"), which is the name of one of Xiamen's two main streets even today.   Gulangyu Islet's Sunlight Rock was command center, and training ground for Koxinga's legendary fighters. He chose as his body guards ("Tiger Guards") only those who could pick up a 600 pound iron lion and walk off with it.

Koxinga's legendary fighters wore iron masks and iron aprons, wielded bows and arrows painted green, and used long handled swords for killing horses—a brilliant strategy he learned in school days while studying about the Great Wall. (The Great Wall was built to keep out not the barbarians but their horses, for while the Tartars were well nigh invincible on horseback, on foot the Chinese easily made Tartar[4] sauce out of them).

On April 21, 1661, Koxinga set sail with 25,000 men and hundreds of war junks to drive the Dutch from Taiwan and return the island to the motherland. This mission cost him his life, but forever endeared him to Chinese on both sides of the straits.   On January 27, 1662, the Dutch surrendered, and Koxinga's men kicked back and played the "Mooncake Gambling Game" (you will too if you're in South Fujian or Taiwan during Mid-Autumn Festival). But patriotism had taken a greater toll on Koxinga's health than piracy had. He died five months later, on June 23.

One Chinese historian noted somberly that Koxinga "died of overwork."

May it be a lesson to us all.

Koxinga's son took over his father's work, but in the end Koxinga's descendants were done in by the descendants of a young soldier that Koxinga wronged and vastly underestimated...

General Shilang (施琅)   The great hero General Shilang was but one of Koxinga's tens of thousands of nameless soldiers when Koxinga ordered him put to death because of some petty infraction or mistake. Shilang escaped, so Koxinga had his entire family put to death instead, but Shilang had revenge (of a sorts) on Koxinga's descendants.

Years later, when the Qing Emperor wanted to oust Koxinga's descendants from power in Taiwan, he asked Premier Li Guangdi (李光地) which general to send. Li Guangdi was from Hutou (湖头) town in Quanzhou's Anxi County (安溪县). You can visit his former home (李光地故居，Li Guangdi Guju) in Hutou. Premier Li knew of Shilang's hatred for the Zheng clan, so he urged the Emperor not to appoint a northerner, who had no feelings about the matter, but to appoint a local who had vested interests—Shilang. Shilang was of course delighted to cross swords with the descendants of the man who had murdered his family, but upon his victory, instead of seeking revenge, Shilang allowed Koxinga's descendants to return to Quanzhou, and to bring back the body of Koxinga to be buried in Nan An. This rare combination of military prowess and benevolence earned Shilang widespread respect and admiration (though once in power, the Shi family turned out to be fairly rascally as well).

General Shilang is also remembered for rebuilding and expanding Nanputuo Temple in 1684, during the reign of Emperor Kangxi. Shilang added the "Great Mercy Hall" for the worship of Guanyin, and changed the temple's name from "Pu Zhao" to "Nanputuo" The large bronze bell was cast during his reconstruction project. On the emperor's orders, Shilang also expanded the Mazu Temple on Meizhou Island because he attributed his success on Taiwan to the sea goddess's intervention. If you'd like to meet the great man, drop by his tomb—not in Nan'an but to the north of Quanzhou, but while we're on this grave subject, I'll throw in a few words about tombs.

Supplement
Tomb Raiders

China's historic tombs are a grave site for anyone expecting to encounter something really historic. Most tombs resemble Lin Lu's resting place, where the emphasis is more on the extinguished gentleman's comfort than on preserving historic relics. Not only have significant tombs undergone complete face lifts, with new stone

Wangchao Tomb

and concrete embellishments, but ancient carvings have vanished. Of course, some are in museums, where they are protected from the elements, vandalism, and theft. But at least the folks in charge should put up a sign (and photos) explaining what used to be on the site, and where it has gone to.

Seeking (futilely) ancient relics at Wangchao's Tomb

Wangchao's Tomb (王潮墓)A Chinese book described the marvelous old stone animals around Wangchao's tomb so I headed Toy Ota down a narrow winding rutted road, through a village and across fields, until I finally found—a new construction site!

The grand arch is impressive, but I climbed all over the site and found nothing but this little chunk off a stone sheep that was cowering in the grass. Disappointing. But Shilang's Tomb turned out to be a site for sore eyes!

All that's left of the Wangchao tomb carvings

General Shilang's Tomb (施琅墓) Just above the Luoyang river, on the 324 highway, a sign for General Shilang's tomb points west. I figured it would be just off the road, but it took half an hour to get there. It turned out to be 15 km away, and I stopped every few minutes to make sure I had not missed it.

Shilang's Tomb

It's not that easy to find, but it is one tomb that is well worth the trip. And judging from the size of the parking lot, the locals are expecting a lot of tourists to visit the final resting place of the benevolent general.

The entire site has obviously been recently renovated, but with style. The stone path leading to the tomb crosses a river and winds underneath shrubs that have been pruned to form shady arches. The general still rests in his old tomb in the back, up against the hillside, his top two wives on either side. Rows of newly hewn

General Garfield

granite officials guard the general's grave, and before them are two rows of original carved animals.

It's a great tomb—and worth the ride to get there. And now we'll head next door to the last Manichean temple on the planet!

Shilang's Tomb

Internet Links for Nan'an

Nan'an government, like most Chinese municipal governments, hasn't put much effort into creating an English website for foreigners, which is understandable. Either they don't bother because their job description doesn't require it, or else they still fancy that the world will come to China regardless, as it did for centuries before the Ming closed the borders (and in that regard they're probably right!). But Nan'an businessmen anxious to take advantage of China's accession to WTO are putting together some very interesting English websites. Input "Nan an" into Google search engine, and you'll come up with some Nan an enterprises' interesting English websites—like Nan An Ceramics, for example:

http://liuquansheng.cnqz.com/qzfair/1e/enterprise.asp?code=F004

Explore online, and then explore onsite, in Nan'an. And then e-mail me with your discoveries for the next addition of *Mystic Quanzhou*.

Notes

[1] Averil Mackenzie-Grieve, *A Race of Green Ginger*, Putnam, London, 1959, p.33.(her account of life in South China in the 1920s).

[2] Xianyou (仙游)Arts & Crafts Town: In addition to marvelous mahogany furniture, they offer Christmas and Halloween figurines, or colorful Grimm's Fairy Tale tea kettles, or faux[2] antique brass photo frames, and great grandfather clocks. the Chen Ren Hai (陈仁海), Vice Director, at (594) 829-5483, Or page him: 129 200-1284.

[3] Beneath the rule of men entirely great, the pen is mightier than the sword; from Edward Bulwer-Lytton's play Richelieu (1839).

[4] Tartar sauce: mayonnaise-based sauce for fish (Tartars were the ferocious Turkish or Mongolians during the Middle Ages).

Chapter 9
Jinjiang and Shishi

My apologies for lumping the two fine cities of Shishi (石狮, Stone Lion City) and Jinjiang (晋江) together in one chapter, but I am not that familiar with those two areas, even though they do have quite a few interesting historical sites. In fact, I have an entire book on Jinjiang sites (which was settled earlier than Quanzhou city proper), but I am personally familiar with Cao'an Manichaean Temple (草庵摩尼教寺) and Chendai Village's Ding Clan Ancestral Temple (陈埭丁氏回族祠堂), both of which we have already visited, and the Ancient Kiln in Cizao (磁灶古窑址) (and we'll look at kilns and porcelain more closely in Dehua). Nevertheless, for the record, here are some key sites:

Cao'An (Manichaean) Temple (草 庵)
Religion of Light

Planet's last Manichaean Temple

Anhai Manichaean Temple, not far from the Sisters-in-Law Tower is the planet's last bastion of the Persian religion Manichaeism, "The Religion of Light" (an esoteric combination of Gnosticism, Zoroastrianism, Christianity, and any other religion that was handy). Mani's followers arrived in China in the late seventh century—just about the same time as their arch rivals, the Moslems and Nestorian Christians.

Mani

The Persian founder Mani (216-276 A.D.) taught that existence is nothing but an eternal battle between good and evil, light and dark. He adopted elements of many religions, reasoning that each contained at least a grain of truth. Mani's malleable metaphysics appealed to St. Augustine, who followed the religion for a decade until his conversion to Christianity.

St. Augustine. The famous Catholic saint and scholar knew too well the eternal battle between good and evil—at least during his hormone driven youth. The intellectual genius partied by night and prayed by day, "God, grant me chastity—but not yet!" After his illegitimate teen-age son died, he entered the Catholic clergy, denounced Mani, wrote a bestselling series of anti-Mani literature, and became a bishop and a saint. The jury is still out on whether he ever achieved chastity, but from the expression on paintings of the man, I doubt it.

St. Augustine

Tang Dynasty Chinese called the increasingly popular religion Moni, Momonifa (Law of Moni), Xiao Moni (Little Moni), Da Moni (Great Moni), etc., and after the Tang it was called Ming Jiao (Religion of Light). For 600 years, this "Religion of Light" found increasing acceptance throughout China, and especially around Quanzhou. In 1954, workers outside Quanzhou's Tonghuai Gate unearthed the tombstone of a high-level Yuan Dynasty clergymen responsible for governing foreign religions, including Manichaeism and Christianity.

Mani's influence in Fujian was so extensive that there is even a small Mani shrine on the peak of Ningde's remote Taimu Mountain (though today it is used by Taimu goddess worshippers).

The growing popularity of the white-robed Manicheans, led by priests wearing violet headpieces, worried Buddhist competitors. The Buddhist history "Fozu Tongji," compiled between 1258-1269, denounced Mani worshippers as vegetarian" devil worshippers. (Odd they should note the vegetarian aspect, since Buddhists too, in theory, avoid meat).

Mani

Mani's minions worried the government—with good reason, it turned out. The politically-inclined Mani worshippers helped overthrow the government and enthrone Taizu, who named his new dynasty "Ming," and then rewarded the Ming Religion by banning it. Supposedly, one reason was that he objected to the Ming Religion having the same name as his new Ming dynasty (which just proves China's early concern for intellectual property rights).

Despite persecution, Mani's religion kept a toehold in Quanzhou, which today boasts the planet's last Mani temple— the "Thatched Nunnery." It was built in 1339, after villagers had spent 26 years carving statues of Mani all over the cliffs of Huabiao Mountain. The artists must not have had a good photo to go by because Mani bears a striking resemblance to standard issue Chinese deities—except that he sports four braided dreadlocks, and has rays of light emanating from behind.

In spite of its uniqueness, some worshippers still think Mani is in fact Guanyin, the popular Goddess of Mercy. I asked a nun if they worshiped Mani or Buddha and she said, "Mani, of course!"
"What's the difference between Mani and Buddha"" I asked her.

She pondered this, then said, "You'll have to ask someone in charge, but there's no in charge at the moment."
Getting There: Special bus to Anhai, get off at Luoshan.
Hours: 8:00 — 18:00   **Phone**: 568-1046

Chendai Village & Ding Clan Ancestral Hall (陈埭丁氏回族祠堂)

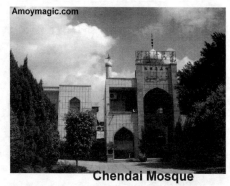
Amoymagic.com

Chendai Mosque

Chendai Village has so many Hui minority folks surnamed Ding that I had to drive at a snail's pace lest I get a Ding in my bumper. Some of the Dings, with their big noses, curly hair and beards, looked like they were ready to burst out in Arabic, not Chinese. Many are not practicing Muslims, but they are fiercely proud of their ancestry, and their Arab forebears' achievements. And modern Ding are quite the entrepreneurs as well! (Turn to "If the Shoe Fits" on the next page).

Mr. Ding Jinhua (丁进华), gave me a tour of the Ding Clan Ancestral Hall (Hui Nationality Exhibition Hall) . This unusual ancestral hall is built in southern Fujian architectural style, but the decorations are Islamic, and it has been carefully designed to resemble the Chinese character Hui 回, with a square hall in the center of a larger square courtyard.

Amoymagic.com

Ding Clan Ancestral Hall (Chendai)

Ding Jinhua

If the Shoe Fits[1] Mainland China produces 80% of the world's sports shoes; 80% of these come from Fujian; most of these are from China's "Shoe Town," Chendai Village!

Not even Imelda Marcos could have dreamed that this sleepy village would end up with over 1,000 shoe enterprises doing over 2 billion Yuan business annually, and have a 22.3 million USD 150,000 sq m. shoe market. Nearby Anhai town is China's largest leather tanning base, and Baiqi is the center for rubber sole production.

Quanzhou as a whole now has over 300,000 people employed in 4,000+ industries producing every make of foreign and domestic shoe possible (excluding, possibly, horseshoes). In fact, Quanzhou produces fully 20% of the world's sports and casual shoes! But it's no wonder. Quanzhou has 100,000 shoe salesmen, and 30 subsidiaries and agencies abroad.

Jinjiang, which produces over 500 million pair of shoes annually, hosted the 1st Jinjiang International Shoe Fair in March, 1999. The four day fair displayed over 5000 kinds of shoes, shoe machines and shoe materials. Over 100,000 people took part in the show, 21 agreements were signed, and sales reached 1.3 billion Yuan. In addition, two Hong Kong specialists gave lectures to 400 business and government leaders.

The latest in computerized design and production technology enables Quanzhou firms to not only keep quality high and costs low but also to go green. Many firms are substituting rubber for azo, and PU for PVC, using benzene-free glue, and replacing white glue laminators with thermosol versions of shoe parts.

For more on the Quanzhou shoe industry, please turn to the supplements at the end of this chapter (p.187~189).

---

[1] Before criticizing someone, walk a mile in their shoes (that way you're a mile away and you've still got their shoes).

Pools   The Ancestral Hall is quite a
museum, with three walls of photographs
and displays behind glass.   The Ding have
prepared a nice little pamphlet on the
history and contributions of the Ding clan
(but no English version).

"Arabic Chinese!"

I tried everything to get a good photo of
the "Hui" shaped hall, including climbing to
the tip top of the Mosque. Mr. Ding solved
the problem by leading me to the market
across the street and borrowing a rickety 30
foot bamboo ladder.   While two Muslims held the swaying ladder from
below, I climbed in, praying silently that they held no historical
grievances against Christians!   But I made it to the roof, and snapped
some good photos of both the hall and the pool in front.   Buddhist
temples have similar pools, which are used for gaining merit by freeing
captive fish, but Muslims have no qualms eating fish.   Perhaps it's the
"Pool for freeing captive pigs?" (After that crack, I know I won't let
them hold any more ladders for me!).

Getting There: Special Bus to Chendai   **Hours**: 8:00 — 17:30

Ding Clan Ancestral Hall

Amoymagic.com

Ding Clan Ancestor

陳埭萬人丁

依瞻代百

Amoymagic.com

Ding Ancestral Hall

On Ancestral Worship

"But the foundations of ancestral worship are not laid on shadowy, visionary soil of myths and legends, but on substantial, solid, historical ground. Ancestral worship has its origin both in the family and nation and is both a family and a national custom. It is as old as the empire itself. Contemporary with the birth of the nation, it has become so interwoven in the warp and woof of its history, that to attempt to disengage the strings would be to destroy the whole fabric... No other one thing in its entire history has tended more to bind this people together or to perpetuate the nation than this universal respect (whether sincere or a sham) for the living and devotion for the dead; and no other one thing has so bound them to the dead past or so diverted their attention from the living future.

Pitcher, *In and About Amoy*, 1912 p.128

Amoymagic.com

Centuries of Dings!

Rizal International Shrine in Jinjiang

In 2002, Jinjiang (a suburb of Quanzhou) invested 10 million Yuan to create the 5-hectare Rizal Memorial Park, with its 18.61 meter high statue of Rizal (much higher than the 12-meter statue of Rizal in Manila). Filipino business leaders invested an additional 2 million Yuan. Filipino House Speaker Jose de Venecia said that China's park was a "great symbol of the 1,000-year-old friendship between our two nations," and, "This Rizal Park in China helps elevate the status of our Philippine national

Rizal Int'l Shrine (Jinjiang)

hero Dr. Jose Rizal as a hero for the whole Asian region."

Rizal's Humble Ancestral Home

The Rizal park will become a must-see for Filipino-Chinese, 80% of whom, like Rizal himself, trace their roots to Southern Fujian. But more impressive than the sprawling (and expensive) park is his tiny ancestral hovel in the little village right

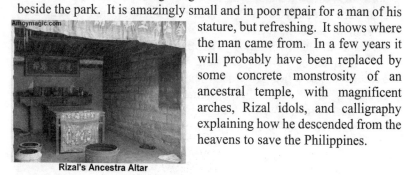

Rizal's Ancestral Home

beside the park. It is amazingly small and in poor repair for a man of his stature, but refreshing. It shows where the man came from. In a few years it will probably have been replaced by some concrete monstrosity of an ancestral temple, with magnificent arches, Rizal idols, and calligraphy explaining how he descended from the heavens to save the Philippines.

Rizal's Ancestra Altar

Jose Rizal
The Filipina Hero from Quanzhou

Rizal

Jose Rizal was born June 19th in Calamba, Philippines, and died December 30th, 1896, in Manila.   This patriot, physician and intellectual was an inspiration to many generations of Filipinos.

Rizal was the son of a wealthy landowner on the island of Luzon, and his mother was one of the most educated Filipino women at that time. Rizal studied medicine in the University of Madrid and became leader of the Filipino students in Spain.   He pursued reform of Spanish rule in the Philippines, though he stopped short of demanding Filipino independence of Spain.   In Rizal's eyes, the Philippine's primary enemy was not Spain, which was undergoing dramatic reform, but the Catholic faction that clung to power in Spain's impoverished colony.

Rizal continued his medical studies in Paris and Heidelberg, and in 1886 he published his first novel, in Spanish. "Noli e Tangere" exposed the evils "of the Catholic friars'" rule much as Uncle Tom's Cabin brought to light the evils of America's slavery.

Rizal returned to the Philippines in 1892 to found a nonviolent reform society, La Liga Filipina, in Manila, but was deported northwest to Mindanao, where during his four years of exile he continued scientific research and founded a school and hospital.

A nationalist secret society, the Katipunan, launched a revolt against Spain in 1896. Though Rizal had absolutely no connections with Katipunan, he was arrested, found guilty of sedition, and executed before a firing squad in Manila. The evening before he was executed, he wrote the Spanish masterpiece, "Mi Ultimo Adios" ("My Last Farewell"), which helped Filipinos realize that there was no alternative to independence from Spain.

Other Jinjiang Sites

Anping Bridge (安平桥) The longest bridge on earth during the Middle Ages, and still the longest stone bridge today! Read up on it in the "Bridges" chapter before strolling across it (but it's a long bridge, so avoid the midday heat). And while you're in Anhai...

Anhai Starry Pagoda (安海星塔, Anhai Xingta) Pagodas don't excite me, usually, but the Starry Pagoda is very distinct. This beautiful red and white four-sided five level pagoda was built in 1629, and is elegant in its simplicity of design.

Anhai Starry Pagoda

Dragon Mountain Temple's 1,000 Handed Guanyin, Goddess of Mercy (龙山寺千手观音, Longshan Si Qianshou Guanyin). Taiwan's famous Longshan Temple is an offshoot of this sprawling Buddhist complex, which was first built during the Sui Dynasty (581-618 A.D.). A millennium later, this was one of the temples that Koxinga's nemesis, General Shilang, helped to renovate. The Guanyin's 1,000 hands, with an eye upon each palm, represent her omnipotence

Dragon Mtn. Temple

and omniscience, but a Buddhist abbot confided to me, "That's just symbolic. If she really had 1,000 hands and eyes she'd be quite a monster!"

Buddha and Relief Cliff Carvings of Nantian Temple (南天寺石佛磨崖石刻, Nantian Si Shifo Moya Shike). Three Cliffside carved stone Buddhas are said to be the crown jewel of Southern Fujian stone carving. Nantian's calligraphy is also popular, particularly the 泉南佛国, Quannan Foguo—"Buddhist Kingdom of Quannan") written by Wang Shipeng (王十朋).

Shishi （石狮, Stone Lion) City

In just over a decade, the 1300-year-old city of Shishi has metamorphosed from a backwater town into a modern center of commerce and industry. Shishi is now the garment capital of Fujian, (中国服装名城, Zhongguo Fuzhuang Mingcheng), considered by some to be the largest garment center in Asia, and host to the Cross-Straits Garment and Textile Expo. Shishi's 5,000 factories+ in the clothing industry did over 7.6 billion Yuan in business in 2001, and the way things are going, businesses likes the 5,000 square meter Xinhu Bra and Underwear Factory aren't going bust anytime soon!

Websites   Unfortunately, Shishi City does not have an English website. The Chinese site is: http://www.chinashishi.com/

If you read Chinese, check out the history page:
http://www.chinashishi.com/history/title.html

Some factory websites are topnotch, and fun to browse. Here are a few:

Shishi Aizimei Garment Co Ltd. http://www.aizimei.com/en/gsjj.htm

Put a spring in your step

Fujian Spring

China Rabbit (locks)

Hare-raising!

China Rabbit Lock Factory is in a key industry:
http://www.china-rabbit.com/company_en.htm

Fujian Spring will put a spring in your step at: http://www.fjspring.com

Wante Battery has a current site, so charge online to: http://www.wante.com

Shishi Xiexing Plastics puts out a broad range of toys, as well as arts and crafts, garments, deng deng. If you can't live without a dancing Santa, plastic scooter, or a toy cobra to frighten your wife (and it will, because we have the real McCoys—or McCobras?—here in Fujian), check out their site:

http://www.xiexing.com/index1.htm

Shishi Tour Sites

Sisters-in-law Pagoda (姑嫂塔)   If you get high on pagodas, visit the 22.86 m Sisters-in-law Pagoda (Gusao Ta), which was built on Baogai Hill (宝盖山) in 1146. On this hill, women used to await the return of husbands and sons from sea voyages.

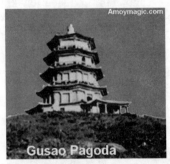

Gusao Pagoda

The Legend of Gusao   Way back in the Song Dynasty, a man sailed forth to Southeast Asia to seek his fortune and promised to return in 3 years. His wife and sister missed him so badly that they piled up stones by the river and watched for him, year after year, but he never returned. The two girls died of grief, and the sympathetic villagers called the rock pile "Sisters-in-Law Tower." And somewhere along the line (1146, actually), the rock pile metamorphosed into a 4-story pagoda that is one of Quanzhou's navigational landmarks even today.

Getting There: Bus from Quanzhou to Shishi
Hours: 8:00 — 17:30   **Phone:** 870-7902

Six Victory Pagoda (六胜塔) is located on the very northernmost tip of a Shishi peninsula. It's tall.

Shishi's Gold Coast Holiday Village （石狮黄金海岸, Shishi Huangjin Hai'an)   The "South Fujian Golden Seashore Holiday Village" is quite a massive undertaking. The first phase includes the Golden Beach Paradise, Yacht Club, Food Plaza, Seaside Resort, and China's largest ocean theme park, the South Fujian Ocean World (which includes an Aquarium, Dolphin

Shishi Gold Coast Holiday Village

Performance Hall, Diving, Underwater Performances, deng deng).

Shishi has miles of beautiful beaches. Yakou (衙口), just a few km south of Shishi, has one of the finest stretches of sand in China. While you're in Yakou, you might want to visit Shi Clan's Ancestral Temple (衙口施氏宗祠).

Getting There: Special Bus from Quanzhou to Golden Seashore
Hours: 8:00 — 22:00 **Phone**: 860-5588, 860-5188

Inway Ni—a young Quanzhou entrepreneur.   Inway, from Anhai, was one of the most driven MBA students I've ever had. Even before graduating he had started several businesses.   But he also knows balance. When his wife had a daughter, he exclaimed to me happily, "Before, I was a full time businessman. Now I'm a full-time father—and part-time everything else!"

Driven, but balanced. *That's* the kind of entrepreneurs our society needs!

A young Quanzhou entrepreneur–and proud father

Supplement

Getting Your Foot in the Door with AIDER

Opportunities are endless in Quanzhou's shoe business, but you can save a lot of time and money with a good go-between to arrange contacts with the more reputable and dependable firms. A good place to start is Fujian's largest footwear exporter, Aider Co., which exports over 300 40' containers annually to customers all over the globe.

Over the past 8 years, Aider has developed a reputation for forging a global network of shoe contacts and building win-win relationships and friendships. And as Aider reps trot around the globe each year to attend shoe fairs, they also give out material to help foreigners better understand Xiamen, Fujian and China. To this end, they bought 2,000 copies of my *Amoy Magic* to give away freely at foreign trade fairs. (Hopefully they're giving away quality literature as well; we want to attract foreign investment, not frighten it off!)

To not only get your foot in the shoe business door, but to make sure it's the right door, contact Aider Co., Ltd. At:
4/F., Foreign Industrial Trade Bldg., North Hubin Road,
Xiamen, China 361012
Tel: 86(592)539-0190   Fax: 86(592)511-0290
Email: john@aider-xm.com   aider@public.xm.fj.cn

Also try some websites like these:
http://www.chinashoes.com/english/site/quanzhou.htm
http://www.china-leather.com/english/market/a7.htm

Supplement

The Quanzhou Tiger

"Asian Tigers" usually brings to mind countries, but Quanzhou City is a tiger in its own right.

During Marco Polo's day, when Zaytun was the start of the Maritime Silk Road and a global commercial and cultural crossroads, the city traded in everything imaginable. Today, the new Quanzhou seems to actually produce about everything imaginable, and has been making great contributions to Fujian and all of China. Over the past two decades, Quanzhou's economy has accounted for ¼ that of Fujian province, and 1.3% that of the entire nation! Private enterprise is playing a pivotal role, accounting for 80% of Quanzhou's GDP in 2000, and thanks to the first Cyber Expo, the entire planet can take advantage of Quanzhou's innovation and production skills.

Cyber Expo—the E-Silk Road　　Quanzhou has so many thousands of enterprises that it can overwhelm the potential buyer or investor. Fortunately, the city has embraced the latest internet technology and practices to create a "Cyber Expo" that is open to the world 24 hours a day, year round. A mere click of the mouse at http://www.qzfair.com or http://www.21marketing.com/qzfair/en/companies.htm opens endless opportunities for partnerships and business deals between thousands of Chinese and foreign firms the world over.

Early on, the Quanzhou government recognized the growing role of e-commerce and net marketing, and in Sep. 1999 initiated the first on-line product expo (the "Never Closing Expo"). The Cyber Expo offers each participant a standard cyber-booth, which includes a home page, sub-domain name, e-mail box, pages for 10 products with text and photos, order-and-pay system, information release system, and net management system. The expo website also offers cyber-booths for companies outside of Quanzhou.

The Cyber Expo's 1st session included 1145 enterprises and over 12,000 projects. The 2nd session, opened Dec. 8, 2000, had 1,500 companies and 20,000 products. The first two sessions resulted in over 1000 orders with a value of USD 17 million. The 3rd session, which opened Nov. 3, 2001, doubled the previous session, with 2,580 companies and over 30,000 products.

The 4th session of "China Enterprises & Products On-Line Expo," (Nov. 2, 2002—Nov. 1, 2003) includes over 3,000 companies from many industries, including textile, shoes & clothing; construction & building materials; arts & crafts; food & beverage; hardware & machinery, petrochemical; electronics & information; tourism & service, and such new ventures as biology & medicine, new materials, environmental protection, and deep processing of farm and sideline products.

The 4th session also held concurrently the 2nd session of China Enterprise Cyber-Marketing Cooperation Conference, and was attended by global business and government representatives, and cyber-marketing experts.

"China Enterprises & Products On-Line Expo" is sponsored by Quanzhou Municipal Government, Fujian Economy & Trade Commission, Fujian Township Enterprise Bureau, and organized by the Quanzhou Township Enterprise Bureau, insuring participants of a top quality program. Contact:

Mail Add.: P.O. Box 98 Quanzhou, Fujian 362000, China
Hot Line: 0595-2105731, 2105730, 2989072
Fax: 0595-2106712, 2989071
Web: http://www.21marketing.net
E-mail: info@qze.gov.cn

China Fair for International Investment and Trade (CIFIT)

CIFIT is the perfect place to make contacts with enterprises from Quanzhou (as well as the rest of China).   China's only investment promotion activity focused on introducing foreign investment, CIFIT not only attracts the planet's top MNCs but has also been responsible for over ½ of foreign investment in China's medium and small enterprises- a total of over $50 billion USD in investment over the past 5 years.

In 2,002, the 6th CIFIT had over 50,000 participants and 10,107 business guests from almost 100 countries and regions.   The 663 contracts signed were worth almost 7.3 billion USD! Speakers at the CIFIT International Forum have included top Chinese leaders, Nobel Prize winners, U.N. officials, and vice premiers of various countries.

Strike gold with CIFIT!   Whether starting business in Quanzhou or anywhere else in China, do yourself a favor and contact:

China (Xiamen) International Investment Promotion Center.

Address: 2/F, Foreign Trade Bldg. Hubin Road N., Xiamen, China 361012.
Phone: 0086-592-5079898-631, or 5068459
Fax: 0086-592-5129898, or 5146205
Website: http://www.chinafair.org.cn
E-mail: 98xiamen@public.xm.fj.cn

Past Quanzhou Attendees of CIFIT have included:

福建惠泉啤酒集团股份有限公司

FUJIAN HUIQUAN BEER INC. LTD.

恒安国际集团有限公司

HENGAN INTERNATIONAL GROUP CO., LTD.

泉州金山石材工具科技有限公司

QUANZHOU JINSHAN STONE TOOLS TECHNOLOGY LIMITED CO., LTD.

泉州市奔达纺织有限公司

QUANZHOU BUNPAT TEXTILES CO. LTD.

泉州市四方数控技术有限公司

SFA NUMERICAL CONTROL TECHNOLOGY CO., LTD.

泉州三盛橡塑发泡鞋材有限公司

QUANZHOU SANSHENG BUBBER PLASTIC FOAMED SHOES MATERIALS CO., LTD.

泉州东科食品有限公司

QUANZHOU DONGKE FOODSTAFF CO., LTD.

Chapter 10

Anxi - Oolong Tea Capital of China

Catering the American Revolution!
Dec. 16, 1773, angry American colonists, disguised as Native Americans, protested against the British tea tax by throwing 342 crates of Anxi tea into Boston Harbor. Thus Anxi helped pave the way for American independence.

Fujian has long been China's tea capital, and Quanzhou's Anxi County the chief source of oolong tea, which at one time was so precious in Europe that only royalty drank it. There are many legends about how tea drinking came about. One says that the Indian monk who introduced Zen Buddhism to China around 530 A.D. cut off his eyelids so he would not fall asleep while meditating, and where the eyelids fell, a plant with leaves shaped like eyelids sprang up. And as luck would have it, these leaves, when brewed, created a stimulating beverage that further helped both the eyelidless master and his pupils stay awake during meditation.

It's a nice story, but I don't see eye-to-eye with it because Chinese drank tea long before Bodhidharma played his eye-opening prank. Many Chinese believe tea drinking began with the "father of agriculture," the almost mythical Emperor Shen Nong (2737-2697 B.C). The first real proof of tea drinking comes from the Three Kingdoms era (222-277 A.D.), and it gradually increased in popularity until the Tang Dynasty, when it became one of the great national pastimes of China—along with poetry, painting, calligraphy, music, martial arts, and all of those other peculiarly Chinese practices that they have perfected over the past 5,015 years.

"Our trouble is that we drink too much tea. I see in this the slow revenge of the Orient, which has diverted the Yellow River down our throats."   J. B. Priestley

Chinese claim that tea not only tastes good but also cures everything from bad eyes to impotence, and was a chief ingredient in the Taoist's elixir of immortality. Tea must also be highly addictive, because we foreign devils fought two Opium Wars and forced the drug on China at gunpoint, for a century, just so we could balance our trade deficit and pay for our tea (and silk, and porcelain, and deng deng).

Tea fanned the flames of American independence in Boston, when colonists threw it overboard during the Boston Tea Party. Tea made the Hatter Mad.[1] But the tea that tantalizes Laowai and Laonei alike nowadays is a far cry from the concoctions Chinese used to brew up!

While Chinese abhor foreigners' adulteration of quality tea with cream and sugar, only 1500 years ago (yesterday by Chinese' standards), the citizens of the Celestial Empire added not just sugar but also rice, ginger, salt, orange peel, spices—even onions! Fortunately, either tea tastes better nowadays or Chinese are inured to it because except for the Tibetans (who still add rancid yak butter), and groups like West Fujian Hakkas (who add pounded meat and veggies!), the only thing added to tea nowadays is pure water, preferably spring water, and if not that, then running river water. And it is served in the elegant yet simple Minnan Tea Ceremony, which many consider to be the precursor of the elaborate Japanese Tea Ceremony. But whereas Japanese have almost made a religion of preparing, serving and sipping tea, the Chinese ceremony has retained a pragmatic simplicity that reinforces my observation that, whereas

Minnan Tea Ceremony

Chinese do tend to stand on ceremony about a lot of things, when it comes to food and drink, their primary aim is to please not protocol but the palate.

Tao of Tea

"Chinese tea lovers never developed an intricate tea ceremony like chanoyu in Japan—which, by the way, they tend not to like because its elaborate stylization is quite contrary to the Taoistic feeling of spontaneity and carefree informality they associate with tea drinking. Nevertheless, there is definitely a Chinese art of tea. It is known as *ch'a-shu.*

"...Tea is at its best when enjoyed in pleasant surroundings, whether indoors or out, where the atmosphere is tranquil, the setting harmonious...Nevertheless, a perfect combination of these five—setting, company, tea, water and tea-things—will fail to work its magic in the absence of the special attitude required to do them justice.

"The key to that attitude is mindfulness...

"When the mind, having freed itself from the trammels of past and future, is fully concentrated on the Here and Now, a whole range of pleasures involving ears, eyes, nose, palate and mood can be enjoyed by two or three people who have come together to make and drink fine tea. However, that enjoyment would fade in the presence of reverential silence, stiff formality or self-consciousness.   John Blofeld[2]

So while you're in Anxi, or anywhere else in Southern Fujian, make sure you take in the Minnan Tea Ceremony. Who knows? It might just cure you of everything that ails you.

Anxi Tea - Elixir of Life?

"We Told You So"...1.3 billion times! Chinese are indefatigable proselytizers, especially of Chinese medicine and tea. If I so much as sniffle, every neighbor, colleague and student on campus accosts me with sure-fire Chinese herbal cures, or compels me to swallow two dozen tiny black pellets made from poisonous toad venom (I kid you not!).

One fellow assured me that a patent medicine cured colds, guaranteed, in 3 days. I asked why, if this was true, his own daughter had fought a cold for a week. He looked at me as if I was proof of why some animals ate their young, and said, "It's a different cold."

Likewise, all of my Chinese friends feel compelled to recite a litany they no doubt learned in school, "Coffee's bad for you but tea is healthy." And how I hate a smug, "I told you so" – especially 1.3 billion of them. Scientists in the U.S. and Japan have discovered that when it comes to fighting cancer, green tea is twice as effective as red wine, 35 times more effective than vitamin E, and 100 times more effective than vitamin C at protecting cells and their DNA. Of course, that's just a restrained Western scientist's viewpoint. Chinese enthusiasts believe the leaf is the long sought after Taoist elixir of immortality.

Anxi Tea Tackles Cancer? Anxi "Chinese Long Life Tea," which won 1st prize in the 2001 Fujian Province Tea Competition, is a popular "medicinal" tea. One website claims this supposedly 2200-year-old tea blend (Anxi wasn't even around 2200 years ago!) regenerates the body at cellular level, attacking free-radical onslaughts, delaying cellular aging and detoxifying the liver, as well as "cure nervous disorders, arteriosclerosis, cardio-vascular failures, premature aging, divers skin conditions including boils, kidney and liver insufficiencies, rheumatoid arthritis, and gout."

As if reading my mind, the author went on to say,

"Regrettably, recalcitrant Western Medicine does not only reject any remedy that lists a too splendid array of claims, but will violently antagonize its spread, branding it as a sheer hoax. Which is the reason why Anxi Tea is still widely unknown in the Western world."

I must rank among the recalcitrant Westerners, because when they claimed that folks in Siberia and Ecuador, as well as China, live up to 120 years because they drink Anxi tea, I wondered how on earth those remote people got hold of it.   Amazon.com, perhaps?

Tea Tours   Anxi tea is big business nowadays, and produced in sprawling tea processing factories, but you can still run across peasant households producing fine teas using time honored methods and homemade machines.   You'll need a local or a guide to help you find them, but it's worth the search, especially when they pull out their cheap little red clay tea sets and, with care and reverence, brew up some of the leaves they themselves have processed.

Your best bet to find such a family is to visit the smaller villages like Longmen (龙门, Dragon's Gate) south of Anxi City proper.   And a suggestion: take a generous bag of candy for the kids and you'll have little friends for life.

Another suggestion: photos!   Every family wants a good photo of the elderly to display after they pass on, but an 8 x 10 costs a small fortune for a peasant household.   As you travel throughout the countryside, take photos, get their addresses, and mail them a copy.   You'll have a friend for life—or maybe even longer!

Fujian China International Travel Service (CITS) provides guided Tea Tours of farms, factories, markets, and the Anxi Tea Museum.

For more info on Fujian CITS, visit **www.citsfj.com/en**
Email: fujicits@public.fz.fj.cn   Phone: (591)337-0110, 337-0071

Touring Anxi   There's more to Anxi than tea! Every time I visit this rural county, I discover new historical, cultural and natural treasures. For instance, I've visited the remote township of Hutou (湖头) at least a dozen times because it's the hometown of Lixi, our baomu (保姆, household helper), who has been with us since 1988 and by now is the 5th member of the family. But the only thing I really knew about Hutou was that it produced South Fujian's best rice noodles (米粉条, mifentiao). Then last year I learned that

Amoymagic.com

500-year-old home! (Anxi, Hutou)

500-year-old courtyard

Lixi was born in a marvelous 500-year-old earthen building. And only last month I discovered that out-of-the-way Hutou was once the home of a Ming Dynasty prime minister!

The deeper I delve, the more fascinating Anxi becomes—and it changes each time I visit, shifting shape with the seasons and the unique cultural and religious traditions and festivals that are celebrated each month (probably each week).

500-year-old man
(Just kidding!)

Amoymagic.com   Amoymagic.com

Half the town turned out for this celebration, and the other half of the town joined in when the foreigner showed up in **Toy Ota!**

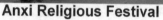

Anxi Religious Festival

"Are we there yet?"

Amoymagic.com

Prime Minister Li Guangdi's Former Residence (李光地故居, Li Guangdi Guju) in Hutou (湖头). I had visited Hutou, our baomu's hometown, a dozen times or more, never imagining that this little backwater was home to an illustrious Qing Dynasty Prime

Qing Dynasty Prime Minister's Home

Minister! Li Guangdi is the man who recommended to the Emperor that Shilang take charge of ousting Koxinga's descendants from Taiwan.

The 3,120 m² home, first built in 1698 (37th year of Emperor Kangxi, in case you're dying to know) is in Hu'er Village, Hutou Township, Anxi County (安溪县湖头镇湖二村, Anxi Xian, Hutou Zhen, Hu'er Cun).

Getting There: Bus to Anxi, change for bus to Hutou Township.
Hours: 8:00 — 17:30 **Phone**: 340-1091

Anxi Confusion Temple
As I noted earlier, the Quanzhou English map has the location for an "Anxi Confusion Temple," (安溪文庙, Anxi Wenmiao), built in 1001 A.D and, according to the literature, "renovated in every generation since then." The present architecture is primarily Qing Dynasty.

Getting There: Bus to Anxi.
Hours: 8:30 — 7:30 **Phone**: 3232553

Qingshui Cliff Temple (清水岩, Qingshui Yan)　　One of China's most picturesque temples, this rambling three-story affair was built in 1083 A.D. right up the side of Penglai Village's densely forested Pengshan Hill, clinging to the hillside rather like the Potala Palace in Lhasa, Tibet. After it burned down in 1277 A.D., monks raised money for the 12-year renovation project that was completed in 1317. When

Qingshui Temple

Amoymagic.com

renovated in 1564 A.D. the temple was home to over 70 monks and nuns.

Qingshui Cliff Temple is a very holy place for Buddhists, and its incense burner has been used to light incense for over 100 burners scattered about Taiwan. A brochure claimed that Qingshui attracts over 600,000 visitors annually, and I can see why. Nice temple—but for me, the biggest attraction is the incredible scenery, and the massive trees. An ancient camphor tree is so large it takes half a dozen people holding hands to reach around it. The ancient sentinel is called "Facing North" because when the tree heard that the good general Yue Fei (岳飞),had been murdered by a treacherous official, the tree held out all its branches to the north to express its sorrow.

Getting there: Bus or train to Penglai Town

Hours: 6:00 — 17:30　　**Phone**: 335-5322

Nine Peaks Cliff Temple (闽南旅游胜地九峰岩) is another of Penglai Town's cliffhanging sites. Built in 1415, during the time of Muslim Navigator Zheng He, it's eight official sites include "Nine Mountains," "Three Tablets," "Lions," and "Huge Rock" (catchy name, that one). The real attraction, for me, is the surrealist scenery, with fog-enshrouded peaks covered with forests of bamboo and camphor, and villages nestled in the valleys. But Chinese like the calligraphy, the number one piece probably being the poem by Ming Dynasty Premier Zhang Ruitu (张瑞图), which reads, "乔木千枝原为一本，长江万派总是同源" "A thousand tree branches have but one trunk, numerous branches of the Changjiang River have but one source." It is particularly appropriate because the little town of Penglai is the source of many streams of Overseas Chinese, many of whom have returned to their ancestral homeland to help rebuild it.

Like Qingshui Cliff Temple, (and just about every other temple in Quanzhou, as well as Christians churches and the Muslim Mosque), Nine Peaks has been renovated with the aid of generous donations from members of Penglai's 100,000+ Overseas Chinese community. They had good reasons for leaving Anxi, and fortunately, even better reasons for returning.

Anxi Fights Poverty Amidst Plenty

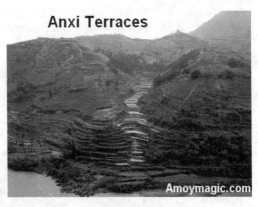

Anxi Terraces

Amoymagic.com

Anxi is the ancestral home for well over 700,000 Overseas Chinese, mainly in Singapore, Indonesia, and Malaysia. Nearly one fourth of Anxi residents have overseas relatives or have lived abroad, and 2 million Taiwanese are of Anxi ancestry. So many Anxi folks cut the apron strings and went abroad because Anxi, though blessed with rich natural resources, was also impoverished.

Anxi has long been famous not just for tea (the best coming from Changkeng, Xiping and Gande) but also for other resources like fruits, minerals, and the forests of Gande, Fengtian, Lutian and Longjuan townships. In Northern Anxi, Jiandou and Weili produce anthracite, Qingyang has manganese, and Pantian mines produce ore with over 55% iron content. The area also has some beautiful crystals.

Anxi Serves "Chicken Soup for the Soul!"

My farmer friends in Anxi's Hutou and Jiandou know that I've collected rocks, gems and crystals since I was a child, and several times have phoned to say, "Professor, we've found another rock for you!"

Amoymagic.com

Anxi style "Chicken Soup for the Soul!"

When I was ill a few years back, two Hutou friends made the long (and costly) trek to Xiamen bearing gifts for both body and soul. They presented me with a live mountain chicken, which they had lugged on the bus for hours (it was for medicinal broth), and a beautiful crystal that a farmer had found in a field and saved for me.

Anxi people are rich indeed—at least in the ways that count.

Though rich in resources, Anxi was until recently impoverished economically. In the mid '80s, Fujian's poorest county was Fu'an; and Anxi was second. The primary cause of their poverty was the county's remote location. Even in the mid 90s, the bus from mountainous Anxi to Xiamen's markets took eight hours. But thanks to new concrete roads, many of them built with the aid of Overseas Chinese, the journey now takes only two hours.

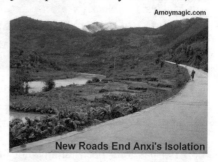

Amoymagic.com

New Roads End Anxi's Isolation

Markets are now mushrooming for Anxi's mountain mushrooms and edible fungi, which are excellent income generators for forested areas because they don't require a large initial investment or long gestation period.

Anxi Anti-Poverty Strategies

My little Anxi friends have a much brighter future today, thanks to Anxi's anti-poverty strategies, which have earned it honor as a model county. Anxi's strategies include measures like providing capital and expertise to impoverished villages, preferential policies for mountain-area development, and an emphasis upon trade and investment.

Amoymagic.com

Little friends in Anxi, Hutou

Anti-poverty teams have helped set up local enterprises, renovated existing ones, helped open mushroom production bases, improved mining operations, raise tea production, combat soil erosion, start fisheries, overcome transportation problems and find markets both in Fujian and throughout China.

After selecting Longmen (龙门, Dragon Gate) Township as a "Science and Technology Anti-Poverty Demonstration Site," The Fujian Academy of Agricultural Sciences sent in experts to improve agriculture and livestock practices. Over a four-year period, household incomes reportedly grew 160%.

The "Oolong Tea Research Institute" and "Oolong Tea Quality Control Center" has helped improve teas, gained footholds in lucrative markets like Shanghai, and exhibited the tea in national and international exhibitions.

Thanks to the concerted efforts of Anxi county, Quanzhou city, and the Provincial Government, Anxi farmers can now have their tea and drink it too! Of course, it helps a lot that Anxi people aren't just waiting for aid but taking matters into their own hands with grassroots movements—like the Longmen bridge project.

Bridges of Friendship   In a vertical province like Fujian, bridges are as important as roads—as Longmen (龙门 , Dragon Gate) discovered.

A few years back the pastor of the Longmen Protestant church (which I've nicknamed the Lighthouse because it sits high above the valley on a hill) told me a typhoon had washed out their bridge, and they could use some helping building a new one.   Otherwise, locals either had to wade the river (quite dangerous at times) or walk several miles to another bridge further south.   And the pastor didn't want just a small bridge for folks to use on Sunday.   "We want a big bridge, that trucks can use. This will help local business as well."

Typhoon washes bridge out

Wade... or walk for miles

Oh me of little faith! I was able to get some friends in America to contribute towards the project, but I never imagined they could build a bridge like he envisioned. And a few months ago, as I was driving past, there it was! Foreign contributions helped a little, but most of the money came from locals, both Christians and nonChristians, working together, to build a bridge of not just commerce but friendship.

Now that's a bridge!

Supplement

The Book of Tea

Kakuzo Okakura's "The Book of Tea," published in 1906, is a marvelous little treatise on the influence of tea on Asian culture, of the differences between East and West, and of why we should try to narrow the gaps. A reviewer wrote of the book, "The words linger with you long after you have finished, and tea, once an ordinary beverage, acquires a soul— a source of peace."

If you enjoy these excerpts, read the entire text, now available online at sites like Abacci Books: **http://www.abacci.com/books/default.asp**

"[Teaism influences] our home and habits, costume and cuisine, porcelain, lacquer, painting—our very literature…the initiated may touch the sweet reticence of Confucius, the piquancy of Laotse, and the ethereal aroma of Sakyamuni himself."

"The average Westerner, in his sleek complacency, will see in the tea ceremony but another instance of the thousand and one oddities which constitute the quaintness and childishness of the East to him…. When will the West understand, or try to understand, the East? We Asiatics are often appalled by the curious web of facts and fancies which has been woven concerning us. We are pictured as living on the perfume of the lotus, if not on mice and cockroaches. It is either impotent fanaticism or else abject voluptuousness. Indian spirituality has been derided as ignorance, Chinese sobriety as stupidity, Japanese patriotism as the result of fatalism. It has been said that we are less sensible to pain and wounds on account of the callousness of our nervous organization!"

"Why not amuse yourselves at our expense? Asia returns the compliment. There would be further food for merriment if you were to know all that we have imagined and written about you. All the glamour of the perspective is there, all the unconscious homage of wonder, all the silent resentment of the new and undefined. You have been loaded with virtues too refined to be envied, and accused of crimes too picturesque to be condemned. Our writers in the past—the wise men who knew—informed us that you had bushy tails somewhere hidden in your garments, and often dined off a fricassee of newborn babes! Nay, we had something worse against you: we used to think you the most impracticable people on the earth, for you were said to preach what you never practiced.

"Such misconceptions are fast vanishing amongst us. Commerce has forced the European tongues on many an Eastern port. Asiatic youths are flocking to Western colleges for the equipment of modern education. Our insight does not penetrate your culture deeply, but at least we are willing to learn. Some of my compatriots have adopted too much of your customs and too much of your etiquette, in the delusion that the acquisition of stiff collars and tall silk hats comprised the attainment of your civilization. Pathetic and deplorable as such affectations are, they evince our willingness to approach the West on our knees. Unfortunately the Western attitude is unfavorable to the understanding of the East.

"Perhaps I betray my own ignorance of the Tea Cult by being so outspoken. Its very spirit of politeness exacts that you say what you are expected to say, and no more. But I am not to be a polite Teaist. So much harm has been done already by the mutual misunderstanding of the New World and the Old, that one need not apologise for contributing his tithe to the furtherance of a better understanding.

"Let us stop the continents from hurling epigrams at each other, and be sadder if not wiser by the mutual gain of half a hemisphere. We have developed along different lines, but there is no reason why one should not supplement the other."

Notes

[1] Mad Hatter: character in Lewis Carroll's classic tale, *Alice in Wonderland.*
[2] Blofeld, John, *The Chinese Art of Tea,* Shambhala, Boston, 1997, Preface.

Chapter 11

Dehua & YongChun

> "The Chinese pottery [porcelain] is manufactured only in the towns of Zaytun and Sin-kalan… The best quality of [porcelain is made from] clay that has fermented for a complete month, but no more… The price of this porcelain there is the same as, or even less than, that of ordinary pottery in our country. It is exported to India and other countries, even reaching as far as our own lands in the West, and it is the finest of all makes of pottery."
>
> Ibn Battuta, Arab Traveler

A Passion for Porcelain

Westerners sold opium, but Chinese trafficked in porcelain, which for the royalty of Europe was more addictive than any poppy product. Thin as eggshells, translucent in sunlight, ringing like a bell when struck, porcelain captured the imagination of Westerners like nothing since Cleopatra's Chinese silk negligees, and was so seductive in its allure that Europeans used "China" as a euphemism for "sex."

Amoymagic.com

A delicate Dehua teaset

Janet Gleeson, author of "The Arcanum,"[1] an absorbing account of the Europeans' pursuit of porcelain, notes that in Wycherley's 1675 play, "The Country Wife," an admirer sees Mr. Horner with Lady Fiddler and begs, "...don't think to give other people china, and me none; come in with me too." After Lady Fiddler comments, "... we women of quality never think we have china enough," the exhausted Mr. Horner says, "Do not take ill, I cannot make china for you all..."

European monarchs gleefully bankrupted national treasuries to satisfy their passion for porcelain. And like monarchs who a millennia earlier were obsessed with spying out the secrets of silk, so Europe's kings were driven to fathom the secret behind porcelain, which like silk was worth more than its weight in gold. Countless potters and scientists were imprisoned until they either produced porcelain or rotted in the attempt. Most rotted. But Quanzhou had the answer.

Zaytun, one of ancient China's two great porcelain centers, was famed for its pure white porcelain, which is considered even today by connoisseur's to be the most sublime of porcelains. Zaytun shipped its celestial crafts, via the Silk Road of the Sea, to the four corners of the earth. Song Dynasty porcelain went for a Song and a dance at home, but it fetched a king's ransom abroad--with good reason.

While Chinese were wielding chopsticks and delicate tableware, my European forebears used fingers and wooden boards, so my ancestors descended upon China in the search for plates, bowls, spoons and spices (medieval Europeans, lacking refrigerators, used Asian spices to doctor spoiled meat).

Wits and Half-Wits Chinese researchers have claimed, in all seriousness, that Chinese are smarter than us barbarians because chopsticks require more dexterity than knives and forks. This may be true. But knife and fork require two hands, whereas chopsticks only need one. Therefore we use both sides of our brain, whereas the chopstick wielders only use one. In other words, our full wit, versus... I rest my case.

About 1,000 years ago (give or take 15), clusters of kilns were located all over Quanzhou, from Hui'an and Jinjiang to Tong An (Tong An and Xiamen were part of Quanzhou back then).   11th century comb-decorated bowls from Tong An have been found in Japan and all over Southeast Asia.

During the Song and Yuan Dynasties, production expanded and gradually moved from the coast to the inland regions of Anxi and Dehua, where output grew fivefold during the Ming and Qing dynasties. Alas, much of the ancient porcelain trade went to pot after the Ming shut China's doors.

Qudougong Ancient Kiln

Qudougong Ancient Kiln

(屈斗宫古窑址)   Since 1949, archeologists have found over 180 ancient porcelain kilns, dating from the ancient Song Dynasty to the recent Qing. These kilns have sure fired up the imagination of guidebook authors, who have written of the 17 chamber Qudougong Kiln, "Such a large-scale kiln of ancient times looks like a dragon crouching on a hill, magnificently." Archaeologists recovered over 6,700 Song and Yuan Dynasty relics from the kiln's 17 chambers.

Dragon kiln

This well preserved ancient kiln, discovered in 1976, is located on the southwest hillside of Mount Pozai, in Baomei Village, Xunzhong Township, Dehua County. Whether you're an expert or a layman, this fascinating site gives insights into Song and Yuan Dynasty ceramic technology and technique. **Getting there**: Special bus from Quanzhou to Dehua
Hours: 8:00 — 17:30 **Phone**: 358-6130

Dehua Porcelain

(see "Porcelain Street 陶瓷街" next page).　I loved the trolls, perhaps because I've got Norwegian blood in me (bitten by a

Mr. Yan Dongsheng

Modern Dehua kilns produce every porcelain product imaginable, provided you've a limited imagination: fine dishes, statues of deities and demons, and gigantic vases big enough to hide in

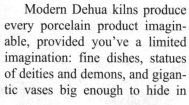

Amoymagic.com

Gramps?

Scandinavian mosquito). I could see a faint resemblance...

Jinhua Porcelain's Manager, Mr. Yan Dongsheng (颜东升), kindly showed us his kilns, workshops and display rooms. Fascinating! Give them a visit. Better yet—give them an order for export!

Fujian Dehua Jinhua Porcelain Co. Ltd, 福建德化锦华陶瓷有限公司
Add.: Huancheng Rd. Dehua 环城路. Ph: 0595 351 8890
E-mail: jinhua@800.com.cn　or: jinhua@pub1.qz.fj.cn

Dehua ducks quack me up

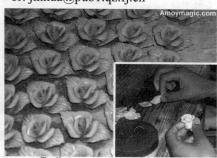

Endless roses -- petal by petal

Porcelain Street (陶瓷街)
The large arch near the river, with the characters 陶瓷街, marks the beginning of Porcelain Street (and probably the end of your budget). This place has great bargains on everything from tableware and statuary to porcelain lamps and waterfalls.

Porcelain Street
Where budgets go to pot

Mr. Lin Shuangyang's Shop

I bought some plates made for export at Mr. Lin Shuangyang's 林双阳 small shop on Porcelain St. Though no one in his immediate family was in the porcelain business, Mr. Lin's cousin had attended the technical school by the ancient Dehua kiln, and opened his own factory in 1973. It wasn't until 1999 that they finally achieved their dream of opening this shop.

Bone Up on blanc de Chine! Learn more about Dehua's exotic porcelain in the fascinating book, "Blanc de Chine—the Great Porcelain of Dehua." Written by Robert H. Blumenfield, an American collector of Dehua's blanc de Chine, the 240 page is available at Ama-

Dishes galore on "Porcelain St."

zon.com for only $52.50 (a bargain, compared with the $75 retail price). Or if you want a real bargain, try "Blanc de Chine: the porcelain of Tehua in Fukien." Amazon.com has two used copies—a steal at only $495 USD.

Dehua Pottery Museum (德化博物馆)　A nice website—but nothing in English, and no address, even in Chinese:

http://www.porcelain–china.com/pottery/dehua169/index.htm

Dehua Cuisine! Dehua has fine food, and even finer prices. Try the Yiyuan Restaurant (益源大酒家)(on Xingnan St.兴南, the same street as "Porcelain Street", but past the river and downtown). We fed quite a crowd, in a private room, for less than 100 Yuan. They offer most of the laowai favorites, but you should also try mountain delicacies like red mushroom soup. Chinese say they cure anemia and replenish women's blood after childbirth because they are red. I doubted that I suffered from either anemia or childbirth, even though my love for Chinese food may cause me to appear like I'm in the second trimester. Still, red mushroom soup is excellent, especially if you have the good fortune to get it right after the mushrooms are picked (they grow only a couple weeks a year, towards the end of August).

Yiyuan Restaurant 益源大酒家 Address: 德化兴南街商业综合大楼 B 瞳2层　Phones: 0595 352-5999 or 352-5998

Some Dehua dishes
(Yiyuan Restaurant)

Pickled beans

Crystal
Dumplings

Fried noodles

Red mushroom
Soup

Amoymagic.com

Incensed in Yongchun （永春）

In China, the drive is always at least as interesting as the destination, and the trip to Dehua is no exception.   The nicely paved concrete road snakes through valleys and past unique villages. The village of Hankou (汉口村) was dusted in crimson, as if the Red Tide had become a red snowfall.

This business is in the red!

Furious ducks (they were seeing red!)

Even the ducks were red. It turned out that red-dusted Hankou was a village of incense makers (and gave a whole new twist to my notion of "Red China")—a tradition they have inherited from their Muslim trader forebears of 800 years ago.

The salvaged Song Dynasty ship on display near Kaiyuan temple is mute testimony to the perils of sea travel even during Zaytun's heyday. The ship was returning to China with many Southeast Asian products. It also had over 2,400 Km of the coveted incense that Muslims were famous for making (I'd have been incensed if my ship of incense sunk). Eventually,Muslims began making the incense right in Quanzhou, and a few centuries later moved to the hinterlands of Yongchun. Today, the Hui minority Pu family still makes incense in a Hankou factory run by Mr. Pu Chongqing (蒲重庆).

Very Red China

Mr. Pu said his Muslim ancestors came to Quanzhou about 1200 A.D..
One of his illustrious extin-
guished ancestors was Mr. Pu
Shougen (蒲寿更), the Chief of
Customs whose wheeling and
dealing accounted for so much of
foreign trade at that time. The
extent of Muslim influnece is seen
in that yet another of his ancestors
was governor of Chongqing, in
Sichuan.

Mr. Pu Chongqing "nose" his stuff

The Pu family's award-winning
Pu Qinglan (蒲庆兰) incense is now as popular overseas as in China,
with annual domestic and foreign sales each equaling about 6-7 million
USD. Visit their factory at 永春县达浦镇汉口村。

Brickmakers Not far from Hankou are fields of domed kilns on both
sides of the highway. I was fascinated at how quickly men fashioned
bricks by hand with wooden forms. Not near as exotic, I suppose, as the
fashionable porcelain up the road in Dehua, but much more practical.

Kilns

No goldbricking here!

Hankou Bridge and Farmhouse!   A beautiful old wooden farmhouse with an enclosed courtyard snuggled up against a hillside, shaded by massive trees.   To get a halfway decent photo I stood in the middle of the highway, one eye on the viewfinder and one on the kamikaze truckers who seemed bent on redressing opium era grievances upon my person.   Finally, I asked a fellow who owned a three storey place across the road if I could take the photo from his rooftop.   He happily agreed, though he could not understand why I'd want to photograph an old house. Why not a new one?

I clamored onto his rooftop and was rewarded with yet another Kodak moment—a panoramic view of the brand new Hankou covered bridge! I had tried to take a photo of it the previous year and couldn't get the right angle. This bridge isn't in any guidebooks, but it should

A classic farmhouse

be, because it proves that bridge building is not a lost art in South Fujian!

Hankou's new bridge is a beauty!

For Whom the Road Tolls   After photographing the bridge
I was on Cloud 9 – until I hit the tollbooth. Every 2-ox town is
building tollbooths and charging going and coming. Fortunately, a few years ago the Provincial government cracked down
on the illegal tollbooths, so at least the remaining highway
robbery is legal.

Actually, jesting aside, I'm thankful for tolls! A decade ago,
roads were so bad that on one trip Toy Ota's shock absorber flew
right off and somersaulted down the road! The motto back then
was, "Fix cars, not roads." But nowadays, thanks in part to tolls,
the new motto is, "Fix roads, not cars," and our beautiful new
roads are easier on cars and passengers both.   So I don't mind
the tolls—but I still have a couple of axes to grind.

One, Toy Ota is charged double on freeways because she is a
van, so the 2 ½ hour drive from Xiamen to Fuzhou sets us back
over $60 USD in tolls! But even that I can deal with. What
really gets me is the towns that build beautiful glass and tile
tollgates with 6 or 8 lanes, then invariably close off all but two.
This is so one person can collect the money and the other 15 can
drink tea and watch the growing line of cars. It almost seems as
if the toll takers aren't going anywhere so they see no reason
why anyone else should either.

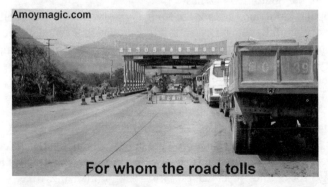

For whom the road tolls

But… it's getting better.   And frustrations aside, Fujian
roads are now some of the best in the country, making travel
faster, fun and safe. So I won't complain.   Much.

Daiyun Mountain (戴云山) "The Ridge of Min" (Fujian Province), this 1856m high provincial-level natural preserve is a delightful place to stroll on a hot summer's day. Attractions include many rare animals and plants (which you won't likely see since they're rare), and Daiyun Temple, which was built in the 2nd year of Taiping in the Liang Dynasty (557 A.D., in other words).

Nine Immortals Mountain, in the Daiyuan range, gets its name from the legend that it was the meeting place for Zhang Guolao (张果老) and eight other immortals. The site has 99 caves, twelve scenic areas, and over 40 calligraphic inscriptions with so many stories behind them that you'd need to be an immortal yourself to hear them all.
>   **Getting there**: Bus from Dehua to Daiyun Village.
>   **Hours**: 8:00 — 19:00 **Phone**: 364-8858

Shiniu (Stone Ox) Mountain (石  牛山)   The 1781m high Stone Ox Mount, in the east of Dehua County, is a circular volcanic basin famous for its many "graceful and marvelous stone caves," though apparently not all are natural. I read that the Stone-Pot Cave of the Lion Cliff was "built" in the South Song Dynasty.
>   Popular attractions include the Ming Dynasty Stone-Pot Temple, and Daixian Waterfall, which descends into a picturesque, winding creek 30 km long. Bamboo raft rides are the best way to emjoy the tranquil scenery.
>   **Getting there**: Bus from Dehua to Stone Ox.
>   **Hours**: 8:00 — 17:00 **Phone**: 362-8118

Lingjiu Rock Temple (灵鹫岩寺) This temple's drawing card is the view. Situated on the northwest of Jiuxian Mountain, the misty scenery changes constantly, but you can always find the 12 official sites of "strange rocks and queer caves" with delightful names like Vulture Rock.
>   **Getting there**: Bus to Dehua bus, and then to Chishui.
>   **Hours**: 6:00 — 17:30 **Phone**: 358-6896

Dongguan Bridge (东关桥). For more on this delightful bridge, please turn to Chapter 6, "Bridges."(p.122)

Amoymagic.com

Bvercaking
Prohibipory

My Favorite Roadsign
Translation:
"Overtaking Prohibited"
Meaning: "No Passing"

Notes

[1] "The Arcanum—The Extraordinary True Story," by Janet Gleeson, reads better than a mystery or thriller as Janet Gleeson recounts the incredible lengths to which Europeans went to discover the "Arcanum" (the secret of porcelain production), and the extremes they went too to preserve the Arcanum once they discovered it. The European's passion for porcelain created an entire industry for corporate espionage, and counter-espionage.

Chapter 12

Quanzhou Cuisine

"One should eat to live, not live to eat!"
Moliere (French dramatist, 1622—1673)

"Moliere never had Chinese food!"
Bill Brown (1956—?)

The earnest Beijing reporter who asked why I moved to China and obtained permanent residence expected a weighty answer on the lines of "To serve the masses," and so I gazed at her solemnly and said, "Because Chinese food is too expensive in America."

There was some truth to that. Let's face it, eating is a big part of life, so we might as well enjoy it, and Chinese are masters of both cooking *and* eating! But Chinese food in China is a far cry from the sweet 'n sour and lemon chicken we get back in America. Chinese delight in eating anything that doesn't eat them first, and they are proof positive that Adam and Eve were not Chinese. Had Eve been Chinese, she'd have tossed the apple and eaten the snake.

Quanzhou cuisine is essentially Minnan (South Fujian) Cuisine, but each area, be it Nan An, Anxi or Hui'An, has its own specialties. The area around Luoyang Bridge, for example, serves succulent oysters so large I could make a sandwich with them. Nan An dishes up excellent leg of lamb with peanut sauce. Anxi's remote hamlet of Hutou is famed for its rice noodles. Quanzhou City itself, located between two rivers and facing the sea, prides itself on rich seafood.

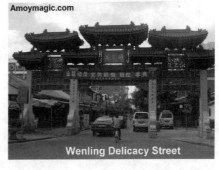
Wenling Delicacy Street

You'd have to travel far and wide to sample them all, but fortunately, Quanzhou City is almost wall-to-wall restaurants. Better yet, the Wenling Delicacy Street packs just about every kind of local food and snack into one 613 meter lane!

A popular breakfast hangout

More fine fare for breakfast

Wenling Delicacy Street(温陵美食街), which which runs north and south between Jinhuai St. and Fengze St., has "more than 130" (probably 131) quaint snack shops and restaurants built with traditional architecture, and offers a wide variety of local Quanzhou snacks and fine cuisine.

One morning, as I happily set forth to enjoy a simple barbarian's breakfast, I was accosted by my kind host and taken to Wenling to feast upon gelatinous sweet potato powder cakes and… read the story on the next page.

Barbarians and Breakfast Americans say the way to a man's heart is through his stomach, and Chinese have certainly won my heart—except with breakfast.

While by noon I can stomach salted minnows, pork fat, deep fried fish lips and sea worms in jellyfish mold, first thing out of bed in the morning my heart and stomach cry out for the familiarity and simplicity of an American breakfast: coffee, eggs, and toast.

The breakfast buffet at Quanzhou's Zaytun Hotel, my Quanzhou home away from home, offers over 60 hot and cold items (yes, I counted!), as well as dimsum, and a chef who will fry up eggs (and then douse them in soy sauce). But I consistently forego these delicacies and ask for eggs, toast, and coffee. This totally bewilders Chinese, for whom any meal must include at least ten courses, half of which are critters seen only on National Geographic channel, the other half being strange veggies harvested from mountains or scavenged from cracks between sidewalks.

After a long day in which I'd had little for lunch and missed supper altogether, I went to bed hungry but happy in the knowledge that next morning the Zaytun Hotel would, albeit begrudgingly, serve me eggs, toast and coffee.

Next morning, just as I was headed to the dining room, my hosts burst upon the scene, exclaimed, "None of that buffet stuff today. We've something special," and led me straight to Wenling Delicacy Street and a big bowl of steaming congealed pig blood soup. Yum.

Amoymagic.com

Pig blood soup for breakfast

Both ends of the streets have memorial gates with inscriptions. The couplet on the Northern gate reads, "Enjoy here the gentle wind and soft moonlight of hometown; raising your glass for a toast, you are intoxicated with love and affection for your townsmen."

Local delicacies include vermicelli paste, white sugar rice cake, Anhai frozen seaworms, fried oysters, rouzong (rice, pork and other ingredients wrapped in reed leaves), Shenhu fish balls, orange rice dumplings, deng deng. And given Quanzhou's location on the sea, between two rivers, seafood occupies a large part of fishy menus. So eat up—and *eat slowly...*

Seize or Savor? Chinese are not only the best cooks but also the best eaters, and their language shows it. A typical greeting is "Have you eaten?" And a common phrase at the table is "Eat slowly!" Where we Americans are always urging the waitress to hurry so we can gobble, guzzle, and get out the door, Chinese are forever admonishing the waitress as she serves up plate after plate, "Slow down! Let us enjoy our food!"

"It is a common pastime, or duty, of Chinese gentlemen to take their birds out for a daily airing" (Franck, 1925)

For an American who lives by the motto Carpe Diem! (Latin for "Seize the Day!") it is hard to handle Chinese who would rather savor a morsel or a moment than seize a day or anything else. Like the fellow above, whether walking their birds or wokking them, they do it slowly. After 17 years in China, I too am slowing down, though I think it is not a philosophical breakthrough but simply the unwinding that accompanies age. Nevertheless, I well relate to the insights shown by Ms. Averil Mackenzie-Grieve, who wrote of her experiences in South Fujian in the 1920s in "A Race of Green Ginger":

Excerpt from "A Race of Green Ginger"
(Ms. Averil Mackenzie-Grieve, Fujian resident in the 20s)

"We could not help contrasting their slow and contemplative savoring of each object of sensuous pleasure with the Western habit of grasping, and discarding half-assessed, a multiplicity of objects or experiences. The Chinese cult of beauty in all forms never lacked elaboration, but it was an elaboration in depth. A spreading downwards of understanding which, like the roots of a tree, nourished and increased pleasure. The foreign traders set themselves to create this Western multiplicity of needs. They had successes chiefly because the Chinese are a practical people and by the end of the nineteenth century, too hidebound by traditions to develop, too arrogant to learn, they had fallen far behind the West, but were shrewd enough, nevertheless, to appreciate the products and inventions of Western science. The foreigners, too, were successful in selling to men and women incapable of making a bad or ugly thing, cheap, mass-produced goods, ugly and badly made, which seemed to us an anomaly until we realize that a Chinese buyer rarely bought foreign goods for aesthetic reasons. The Chinese admired neither the appearance of the Westerners nor that of their goods. They were, however, fascinated by the mechanical ingenuity of the West. The Western merchants found a market, too, among the poor and unlettered, to whom the opening of the Treaty Ports brought, if not an increase in prosperity, at least a raising of subsistence level. Inland, however, the Chinese were still extremely conservative.

'If you want to make money out here, you've got to make the Chinese want things, and want 'm so badly that they get so's they bloody well can't do without 'em'; Mr. Tulser poured more brandy into his beer. 'That's the secret.' ..

"I surveyed the long and, to me, still bewilderingly complex civilization of the Chinese, and said, 'I should have thought the Chinese wanted enough things.'

" 'Ah, but,' Mr. Tulser pointed a knowing, nicotine-stained finger, 'you've got to make 'em want the things you want 'em to want. Why, many's the time as a young ''un—believe it or not—I've stood on a soap box in a village up-country teaching the Chinese how to smoke cigarettes. Never seen 'em before—and look at 'em now; smoke like lime-kilns…. And are they grateful?… ''Nough to drive you to drink, isn't it?'"

Master Chef Zhong takes food seriously!

Zhong Mingxuan (钟明选) The Master of Quanzhou Cuisine

I was very fortunate to enjoy a meal prepared by Quanzhou's most celebrated chef, Mr. Zhong Mingxuan.   Mr. Zhong is the host of Quanzhou TV's popular Minnan Cuisine program, and has been filmed by TV crews from Hong Kong, Macao, Taiwan and Zhejiang Province.

All of the guests clamored for Chef Zhong to make an appearance in their private dining rooms, so he would chat a few minutes, race out, race back in, race back out again—but I gradually managed to pin down a picture of the man's career, which is being carried on by his 31 and 27 year old sons, Zhong Yichuan (钟驿川) and Zhong Yidong (钟驿东).

Chef Zhong, now aged 55, has been whipping up prize-winning Quanzhou cuisine since 1965, but he doesn't stay at one place long. "I don't go to the best places but to the places that need help," he said. "I need a challenge." So either I was eating at a less than best place or this man was a miracle worker because he'd only been at this restaurant for two months.

"I don't like to just rely on tradition," Chef Zhong said. "I'm bold. I like to experiment. Xiamen was the earliest to introduce foreign flavors, like garlic. Quanzhou leads in Minnan cuisine, but Xiamen is second, and Zhangzhou third."

I don't know if his dishes were classics or just experiments to pawn off on foreigners, but each one was so tasty I was hard put to photograph them before devouring them. I especially enjoyed Minnan spring rolls (闽南薄饼, minnan baobing), chicken rolls (鸡圈, jiquan), silk gourd gum soup (丝瓜蛏根汤, sigua chengen tang), sesame sweet potato cakes (芝麻地瓜饼, zhima digua bing—which differ everywhere), and Baoshao Tofu (包烧豆腐, baoshao doufu). But I thought I had died and gone to heaven when I got a taste of Osmanthus Crab (桂花蟹, guihua xie), which looked like scrambled eggs and crab, but tasted like nothing in this world.

A crabby dish

Osmanthus crab is heavenly!

Through Dante's Inferno...   **...to 7th Heaven!**

Minnan spring rolls are quite unlike any others in China. Diners are often given the various veggies, meats, sauces and peanut powder on saucers, and they assemble their own mix and wrap it in paper thin soft white wrappers.   Now that I'm used to this, I prefer them to the more common deep-fried spring rolls because they aren't drenched in oil.

For now, you can catch Chef Zhong performing nightly at the Huxin Hotel (泉州湖心大酒店）

Address: Central section of Huxin
   Street (湖心街中段).
Phone: 228-2888 ext. 3397

Alan Smith assembles a Minnan Spring Roll

Quanzhou
Cuisine

Some favorite Quanzhou Cuisine dishes (from Chef Zhong, and also the Zaytun Hotel)

Fish in Rice Krispies (麦香银卷鱼, maixiang yinjuan yu) –Absolutely my favorite! (They said it was crisped wheat, but I think it was rice).

Fish 'n crispy rice

Tofu (一品豆腐, yiping doufu).   There are few things healthier or more versatile than doufu, and this is one of the best dishes I've had. Also try the incredible baoshao tofu.

Baoshao Tofu (excellent!)

Pickled red veggies with preserved egg (苋菜, xiancai). It tastes a lot better than it looks!

Beef and Oyster Sauce (蚝油牛肉, haoyou niurou).   Pork is king in China, so beef is sometimes not up to snuff. I've suspected some beef as being sole food (recycled shoe soles). But Zay-Zaytun's beef melts in your mouth.

Shark Lips (鱼唇煲, yuchun bao). I told them not to give me any lip but they did anyway—shark lips! It wasn't that bad, actually. Not lip smacking, but tasty. They're sort of chewy, like rubbery fish jello.

Shark lips!

Pickled Beans (豇豆, Jiangdou) – a tasty little appetizer.

Fried Veggie buns (煎包, Jianbao). Excellent!

Lamb ribs in foil (手撕羊排). Delightful; reminds me of Mongolian lamb, but without the baked sheep's head staring me in the face.

Quanzhou Noodles (卤面). Nice way to end a meal! (Long noodles symbolize long life).

Home Cooked Quanzhou Style Minnan Cuisine

Try your hand at these recipes!

Swimming Crab Dish—the #1 dish (in my eyes, at least—and stomach too). Steam live crabs, then shell them and remove the inedible parts (I was surprised to learn that Chinese deemed anything inedible). Cut the pork, water chestnuts, scallion stalks and bamboo shoots into 1 inch strips and mix with beaten eggs and salt. Thoroughly mix in the shelled crabs, stir-fry in hot oil with oil and shredded ginger. After frying, add Shaoxing wine.

Coral Prawn: I'm not sure how they corral coral prawns, but they're heavenly. Clean live prawns, deep-fry quickly, and season with diced ginger, garlic, sugar, thick Minnan chili sauce, scallions, Shaoxing wine, and clear broth. Sprinkle with pepper powder and sesame oil. Devour—slowly, if possible. If not, at least take a photo so while they're digesting you can remember what they looked like.

River Eel: I was glad my hosts bore me no eel will then they served this excellent dish. Clean Jinjiang River eel and cut into two inch slices. Marinate eels for one hour in a blend of salt, crushed ginger, and wine. Deep fry the eel slices and add oil, sugar, soup-stock, small pieces of pork, soy sauce, and Shaoxing wine. Steam in a steamer (duh!), then spray with sesame oil.

Steamed Perch: I was perched on the edge of my chair waiting for this one! Select a two pound or larger perch and then scale and clean it. Place on a large bamboo steamer with small chunks of pork, slices of winter bamboo and ginger, shoots, winter mushrooms, scallion stalks, and some salt and water. Steam on high flame for 20 minutes, and then remove scallion stalks and ginger slices (personally, I like to eat these).

Fried Red Crabs: The crabbiest diner mellows after feasting on red crabs, which are harvested in the winter. Shihu of Hanjiang (Quanzhou

Bay) produces the best red crabs. Pickle large red crabs (at least one pound) in sorghum liquor and then wrap in fatback. Place the lard-wrapped red crabs upside down in a pot with ginger slices and sorghum liquor and allow them to steam for ten minutes. When done, remove the fatback, clean the crabs, and cut each crab into eight slices.

More Minnan Cuisine (borrowed from "Amoy Magic").

Spicy Fried Rolls   Wrap these ingredients in a round sheet of dried tofu: cubed pork, fish meat, onions, water chestnuts, soy sauce, five spices, sweet potato starch. Deep fry, cut in slices, serve.

Minnan Spring Rolls   These delightful delicacies are like a Minnan version of a Mexican burrito. Buy spring roll wrappers at the market, and for the filling, make a mixture of shredded carrots and bamboo shoots, green peas, shredded meats and shrimp, tofu, and anything else that strikes your fancy or wanders in off the street. Cook it well, add salt and soy sauce, and wrap in spring roll wrappers, along with a little mustard, chili sauce, plum sauce, scrambled eggs, leeks, and Chinese parsley (coriander). Enjoy.

Oil-Scallion Cake   Add fish meat to diced pork and water chestnuts, then add a little sweet potato starch, some scallions, a dash of Five Spice, and some sugar and salt. Form into balls and coat with rice starch in bowls and steam. Let cool, and sprinkle with your favorite Chinese condiments (chili paste, pickled radish, deng deng).

Tosun (Jelly Fish and Sea Worm)   This is Xiamen's number one specialty. It's also the one thing I can't handle—but you haven't lived until you at least try.

These culinary delights are dug from the mud on the beach. Enough said there. Wash the Tosun (jelly fish) clean and stew over a slow fire until the gelatine dissolves. Pour soup into cups and allow to cool into a jello-like substance (somewhere along the line adding seaworms).

Force down with Chinese chili sauce, mustard sauce, vinegar.

Fried Squid Our favorite! Clean squid thoroughly and soak in clear water for a couple of hours, then cut it into thin slices and score with intersecting diagonal cuts. Fry the squid with bamboo shoots, scallions, tomato, sugar and vinegar until they roll up into a tube shape. (Don't overcook or they'll have the texture of rubber grapes).

Fried Oysters (sort of an oyster-egg pancake) Dip oysters in sweet potato starch, add soy sauce, and fry. Pour beaten eggs on the mixture and continue to fry until done. Add Chinese parsley (coriander); eat with mustard or chili sauce.

Stir-Fried Rice Noodles Deep fry rice noodles (a vermicelli type noodle) until golden, then rinse in boiled water to remove grease. Stir-fry shredded pork, fish, mushrooms and bamboo shoots in peanut oil and add chicken bouillon, Shaoxing wine, and salt. Add the noodles and serve hot. Awesome.

Zongzi My wife's favorite! These are pyramid-shaped dumplings of glutinous rice and other ingredients, wrapped in bamboo leaves. Originally served on the Dragon Boat Festival, nowadays they are found year round. Make your own by stir frying glutinous rice, pork, chestnuts, mushrooms and shrimp (some use red beans). Wrap them with bamboo leaves into a pyramid shape, tie them, then braise them in a soup until well done. Dip the zongzis in a mixture of soy sauce and garlic.

Zongzis (Sue's favorite)

Quanzhou Snacks

Oyster Chowder: a hearty porridge made of glutinous rice, fish, pork, oysters, soy sauce, and pepper, often accompanied with youtiao (twisted deep-fried dough sticks) or turnip cakes.

Quanzhou Beef is served in shops around town, two of the best just around the corner from the 4-star Quanzhou hotel.

Amoymagic.com

A local favorite: Quanzhou beef

Stuffed Fishballs (another of my favorites, some say the best come from the walled city of Chongwu). Finely diced pork, dried shrimp and water chestnuts are mixed, wrapped in a coating made from fresh fish and starch, and boiled until done. Serve with mashed garlic and pepper in soy sauce.

Somethin' fowl's afoot.

Pickled Chicken Feet. I was sure somethin' fowl was afoot when they served up these fellows, but locals sure love them—second only to jellied duck webs.

Turnip Cakes (my favorite): powdered turnip, rice and flour are mixed, a dash of salt is added, excess moisture pressed out, cut into slices, and deep fried.

Steamed sponge cakes are made from rice flour and sugar, which is fermented and then steamed in bowls.

Fried Sesame cakes: glutinous rice paste is stuffed with a blend of sesame seeds, peanuts, sugar, and diced winter squash, then deep fried.

Orange Cakes: powdered glutinous rice is steamed, sugar is added, and the mixture is molded into different shapes.

Sesame Cakes: fried sesame cakes are wrapped with orange cakes, steamed, and sprinkled with sesame seeds.

Peanut Soup: a favorite in Southern Fujian, where folks have long worked for peanuts, this is simplicity itself to make. Simply boil peanuts to form a milky soup, and serve up at the end of the meal—either with, or in place of, the fresh fruit platter.

More recipes? **The Chinese Garden** has more great recipes from all over China. Download beautiful color photographs and recipes, in either Chinese or English, from http://www.chinese-garden.com

Dictionary of Common Chinese Foods ...

One of the biggest problems foreigners have in China is ordering food from Chinese menus, so I spent ages compiling a dictionary of Chinese food for "Amoy Magic," which I offer for your use here as well...

Getting a Handle on Chinese Food

It is a sad truth, but we have lost the faculty of giving lovely names to things. Names are everything. I never quarrel with actions. My one quarrel is with words... The man who could call a spade a spade should be compelled to use one. It is the only thing he is fit for.   Oscar Wilde

Chinese prefer strange and exotic foods, but failing that, they give common foods strange and exotic names.   They pass off plain chicken as "Phoenix Breast," or duck eggs as "Lotus Eggs."   And the famous "Monk Climbing the Wall" soup has neither monk nor wall.   I hope.

The playwright who quarreled with words would have appreciated these offerings from Chinese menus:

Silver Fish Wrapped in Snow, from Beijing, is neither winter precipitation nor the ornery bugs that ate holes in my wool Scottish tie. It is simply cooked macaroni fried in whipped egg white.

Chicken in a Lantern, also from Beijing, is cooked chicken and vegetables wrapped in clear cellophane and tied with a ribbon.

Phoenix Breast, from Sichuan, is not the legendary Egyptian fowl but plain old chicken breast, like you get for 69 cents a pound at Safeway.

Lotus Eggs are not the lotus' source; they're just chicken eggs.

Dragon and Phoenix Ham, from Sichuan, is naught but duck, pork, water chestnuts, chicken wing bones, ham and white bread – mixed and fried. (So who was the dragon?).

Steamed Dragon's Eye rolls, from Sichuan, are strips of pork rolled around red bean paste, topped with a cherry, and served on glutinous rice.

By the time I've worked my way to a menu's soup section and come across, "Bright Moon in a River" and "Buddhist Monk Climbing the Wall," I'm ready to climb the wall myself.   But it's worth the climb.   The elegantly named dishes are invariably just as elegantly prepared and served, and well worth the wait.

To make your life easier, we offer the Laowai's Lexicon of Chinese Cuisine.

If you can't pronounce any of the dishes, **just point!**

Chinese Cuisine

中餐 **(ZHONGCAN)** Chinese Food　西餐 (XI CAN) Western Food

PORK 猪肉(ZHU ROU)

青椒肉丁 (QINGJIAO ROU DING) Stir-fried Pork & Green
Peppers
青椒塞肉 (QINGJIAO SAI ROU) Steamed Green Peppers Stuffed
with Minced Pork
炒肉片 (CHAO ROU PIAN) Stir-Fried Pork Slices
木须肉 (MU XU ROU) Stir-fried Pork Slices & Eggs
糖醋里脊 (TANG CU LI JI) Sweet & Sour Pork　(Boneless)
糖醋排骨 (TANG CU PAI GU) Sweet & Sour Pork Rib
红烧猪肉(HONGSHAO ZHU ROU) Braised Pork with Brown Sauce
栗子红烧肉(LI ZI HONG SHAO ROU) Braised Pork with Chestnuts
冬笋肉丝(DONG SUN ROU SI) Stir-fried Shredded Pork & Bamboo
Shoots
炸丸子(ZHA WAN ZI) Fried Pork Balls

BEEF 牛肉 (NIU ROU)

咖喱牛肉 (GA LI NIU ROU)　Beef & Curry
炒牛肉片 (CHAO NIU ROU PIAN) Stir-fried Sliced Beef
红焖牛肉 (HONG MEN NIU ROU)　Braised beef in Soy Sauce
蚝油牛肉 (HAO YOU NIU ROU) Braised Beef in Oyster Sauce
红烧牛腩(HONG SHAO NIU NAN)Braised Beef Tenderloin Chunks
in Soy Sauce
青椒牛肉(QING JIAO NIU ROU) Beef & Green Peppers

CHICKEN 鸡 (JI)
果仁鸡丁(GUO REN JI DING) Stir-Fied Diced Chicken and Peanuts
青椒鸡丁 (QING JIAO JI DING) Stir-Fried Chicken with Green Peppers
炒鸡片 (CHAO JI PIAN)　Fried Chicken Slices
冬笋鸡片(DONG SUN JI PIAN)　Stir-fried Chicken and Bamboo Shoots
糖醋鸡条 (TANG CU JI TIAO)　Sweet 'n Sour Chicken Strips
双冬鸡条 (SHUANG DONG JI TIAO) Braised Chicken with Mushrooms
& Bamboo Shoots
栗子鸡 (LI ZI JI) Stewed Chicken and Chestnuts

油豆腐鸡 (YOU DOU FU JI) Stewed Chicken with Fried Tofu
油酥鸡 (YOU SU JI) Crispy Fried Chicken
蚝油手撕鸡 (HAOYOU SHOUSI JI) Fried Shredded Chicken in Oyster
　　　　Sauce
炸鸡 (ZHA JI) Fried Chicken
炸纸包鸡 (ZHA ZHI BAO JI) Paper Wrapped Fried Chicken
炸鸡肉串 (ZHA JI ROU CHUAN) Fried Chicken Shish-ka-bob
烤鸡 (KAO JI) Roast Chicken
冬笋门胗 (DONG SUN MEN ZHEN) Stewed Gizzards & Bamboo
　　　　Shoots
草菇蒸鸡 (CAO GU ZHENG JI) Steamed Chicken & Straw Mushrooms
荷包栗子鸡 (HE BAO LI ZI JI) Steamed Chicken Stuffed & Mushrooms
芝麻鸡 (ZHI MA JI) Sesame Chicken
咖喱鸡 (GA LI JI) Curried Chicken
红烧鸡翼 (HONG SHAO JI YI) Braised Chicken Wings with Brown
　　　　Sauce

DUCK　鸭 (YA)

烤鸭 (KAO YA) Roast Duck
北京烤鸭 (BEIJING KAO YA) Beijing Duck
蚝油扒鸭 (HAO YOU PA YA) Braised Duck with Oyster Sauce
红烧全鸭 (HONG SHAO QUAN YA) Whole Braised Duck in Soy Sauce

EGG DISHES 蛋 (DAN)

炸象眼鸽蛋 (ZHAXIANG YANGE DAN) Fried Pigeon
　　Eggs & Minced Meat
火腿蒸蛋 (HUO TUI ZHENG DAN) Steamed Ham and Eggs
肉末鸡蛋 (ROU MO JI DAN) Minced Pork Omelette

OTHER FOWL PLAY

核桃禾花雀 (HE TAO HE HUA QUE) Spicy Sparrow &
　　　　Walnuts
炒鸽松 (CHAO GE SONG) Fried Minced Pigeon Meat
烤酿禾花雀 (KAO NIANG HE HUA QUE) Baked Stuffed
　　　　Sparrow
鸡茸燕窝 (JI RONG YAN WO) Braised Bird's Nest with Minced Chicken

MUTTON 羊肉 (YANG ROU)

红烧羊肉 (HONG SHAO YANG ROU) Braised
   Beef with Soy Sauce
烤羊肉 (KAO YANG ROU) Roast Mutton
烤羊排 (KAO YANG PAI) Roast Mutton Chops
芝麻羊肉 (ZHI MA YANG ROU) Fried Mutton
   with Sesame

MISCELLANEOUS CARCASSES

炒兔片 (CHAO TU PIAN) Stir-Fried Rabbit
红烧鹿肉 (HONG SHAO LU ROU) Braised Deer with Brown Sauce
炸田鸡腿 (ZHA TIAN JI TUI) Fried Frog Legs

SEAFOOD 鱼 (YU)

糖醋鱼片 (TANG CU YU PIAN) Sweet and Sour Fish
糖醋石斑鱼 (TANG CU SHI BAN YU) Sweet 'n Sour Garoupa
炒鱼片 (CHAO YU PIAN) Stir-Fried Fish Strips
炸鱼条 (ZHA YU TIAO) Deep Fried Fish Strips
酥炸鱼条 (SU ZHA YU TIAO) Crispy Fried Garoupa Slices
炸鱼 (ZHA YU) Deep-Fried Fish
炸桂鱼 (ZHA GUI YU) Deep-Fried Mandarin Fish
蒸鲜鱼 (ZHENG XIAN YU) Steamed Fresh Fish
蒸桂鱼 (ZHENG GUI YU) Steamed Mandarin Fish
红烧鱼 (HONG SHAO YU) Braised Fish with Soy Sauce
红烧鳗鱼 (HONG SHAO MAN YU) Braised Eel with Soy Sauce
红烧鲤鱼 (HONG SHAO LI YU) Braised Carp with Soy Sauce
清炖甲鱼 (QING DUN JIA YU) Braised Turtle in Clear Broth
炒鱿鱼 (CHAO YOU YU) Stir-Fried Squid
炸鱿鱼 (ZHA YOU YU) Deep-Fried Squid
蚝油鱼唇 (HAO YOU YU CHUN) Braised Fish Lips in Oyster Sauce

SHRIMP 虾 (XIA)

盐水虾 (YAN SHUI XIA) Boiled Shrimp
清炒虾仁 (QING CHAO XIA REN) Stir-fried Shelled
   Shrimp
油炸虾丸 (YOU ZHA XIA WAN) Deep-Fried Shrimp Balls
红烧大虾 (HONG SHAO DA XIA) Braised Prawns in Brown Sauce

炸大虾 (ZHA DA XIA)   Deep-fried Prawns
炸烹大虾 (ZHA PENG DA XIA) Fried King Prawns
炸虾串 (ZHA XIA CHUAN) Fried Prawn Shish-ka-bob
炸虾饼 (ZHA XIA BING) Fried Prawn Cutlets
煎酿大明虾 (JIAN NIANG DA MING XIA) Fried King Prawns in
        Soy & Ginger Sauce
炸竹笋脆虾 (ZHA ZHU SUN CUI XIA) Fried Prawns & Bamboo Shoots
炸虾球 (ZHA XIA QIU) Fried Prawn Balls

CRAB 蟹 (XIE)

蒸螃蟹 (ZHENG PANG XIE) Steamed Crab
炒蟹肉 (CHAO XIE ROU) Stir-Fried Crab Meat
奶汁蟹肉 (NAI ZHI XIE ROU) Stir-Fried Minced Crab & Cream Sauce

OTHER SEA CRITTERS

红烧海参(HONG SHAO HAI SHEN) Braised Sea Cucumbers in Brown
    Sauce
虾仁海参 (XIA REN HAI SHEN) Stewed Sea Cucumbers
with
      Shrimp
油爆干贝 (YOU BAO GAN BEI) Fried Dried Scallops with
      Vegetables
白汁干贝 (BAI ZHI GAN BEI) Stewed Dried Scallops in White Sauce
面拖牡蛎 (MIAN TUO MU LI) Fried Oysters
蚝油焖鲍鱼 (HAO YOU MEN BAO YU) Stewed Sliced Abalone in
      Oyster Sauce
红烧鲍鱼 (HONG SHAO BAO YU) Braised Abalone in Brown Sauce
冬菇鲍鱼 (DONG GU BAO YU) Braised Abalone & Black Mushrooms

VEGGIES 蔬菜 (SHU CAI)

炒素菜 (CHAO SU CAI) Stir-Fried Mixed Vegetables
菜心扒鲜菇 (CAI XIN PA XIAN GU) Stir-Fried Vegeta
    bles & Mushrooms
炸茄盒肉 (ZHA QIE HE ROU) Fried Eggplant Stuffed with Pork
醋熘白菜 (CU LIU BAI CAI) Stir-Fried Chinese Cabbage
油焖笋 (YOU MEN SUN) Braised Bamboo Shoots
烩鲜菇蔬菜 (HUI XIAN GU SHU CAI) Stewed Fresh Mush
      rooms & Vegetables

炒香菇笋片(CHAO XIANG GU SUN PIAN) Stir-Fried Mushrooms
        & Bamboo Shoots

TOFU (BEANCURD) 豆腐 (DOU FU)

炒豆腐 (CHAO DOU FU) Stir-Fried Tofu
炸豆腐 (ZHA DOU FU) Deep-Fried Tofu
红烧豆腐 (HONG SHAO DOU FU) Braised Tofu in Brown Sauce
素什锦豆腐 (SU SHI JIN DOU FU) Braised Tofu with Mixed Vegetables
红烧什肉虾仁豆腐 (HONG SHAO SHI ROU XIA REN DOU FU) Braised
                 Bean Curd, with Shrimp, Meat & Brown Sauce
鱼脊肉酿豆腐 (YU JI ROU NIANG DOU FU) Steamed Tofu Stuffed
         with Minced Fish
猪肉酿豆腐 (ZHU ROU NIANG DOU FU) Steamed Tofu Stuffed
        & Minced Pork
油豆腐嵌肉 (YOU DOU FU QIAN ROU) Fried Tofu Stuffed and
         Minced Pork
蚝油豆腐 (HAO YOU DOU FU) Tofu in Oyster Sauce

SOUPS 汤 (TANG)

鸡茸玉米汤 (JI RONG YU MI TANG) Chicken Corn Soup
牛肉汤 (NIU ROU TANG) Beef Soup
鸭汤 (YA TANG) Duck Soup
三鲜汤 (SAN XIAN TANG) Fish, Shrimp & Pork Ball Soup
鲍鱼鸡片汤 (BAO YU JI PIAN TANG) Abalone & Chicken Soup
酸辣汤 (SUAN LA TANG) Hot & Sour Soup
燕窝汤 (YAN WO TANG) Bird's Nest Soup
豆腐汤 (DOU FU TANG) Tofu Soup
蛋豆腐汤 (DAN DOU FU TANG) Tofu & Egg Flower Soup
鸡蛋汤 (JI DAN TANG) Egg Drop Soup
锅巴口蘑汤 (GUO BA KOU MO TANG) Mushroom & Crispy Rice Soup
干贝汤 (GAN BEI TANG) Dried Scallop Soup

ON A ROLL

馒头 (MAN TOU) Steamed Bun
素菜包子 (SU CAI BAO ZI) Steamed Bun Stuffed with Vegetable
肉包子 (ROU BAO ZI) Steamed Bun Stuffed with Minced Pork
饺子 (JIAO ZI) or 水饺 (SHUI JIAO) Boiled Stuffed Chinese
         Dumpling

蒸饺 (ZHENG JIAO) Steamed Jiaozi (Dumpling)
三鲜蒸饺 (SAN XIAN ZHENG JIAO) Steamed Seafood Jiaozi
锅贴 (GUO TIE) Lightly Fried Jiaozi
小笼包 (XIAO LONG BAO) Small Dumplings in Bamboo Steamer
春卷 (CHUN JUAN) Deep Fried Spring Roll
葱花饼 (CONG HUA BING) Pancake with Green Chinese Onion
肉饼 (ROU BING) Fried Meat Pie
烧饼 (SHAO BING) Baked Sesame-Seed Cake
米糕 (MI GAO) Steamed Rice Cake
油条 (YOU TIAO) Deep-Fried Dough Sticks (breakfast food)

NOODLES 面条 (MIAN TIAO)
拉面 (LA MIAN) Hand pulled noodles (usually Muslim)
炒面 (CHAO MIAN) Fried Noodles
牛肉炒面 (NIU ROU CHAO MIAN) Beef Fried Noodles
虾炒面 (XIA CHAO MIAN) Shrimp Fried Noodles
海鲜炒面 (HAI XIAN CHAO MIAN) Seafood Fried Noodles
蔬菜炒面 (SHU CAI CHAO MIAN) Fried Noodles and Vegetables
方便面 (FANG BIAN MIAN) Instant Noodles
米粉条 (MI FEN TIAO) Rice-Flour Noodles
肉丝拌面 (ROU SI BAN MIAN) Noodles with Shredded Pork
汤面 (TANG MIAN) Noodle Soup
三鲜汤面 (SAN XIAN TANG MIAN) Seafood Noodle Soup

FRIED RICE 炒饭 (CHAO FAN)
猪肉炒饭 (ZHU ROU CHAOFAN) Pork Fried Rice
牛肉炒饭 (NIU ROU CHAOFAN) Beef Fried Rice
鸡炒饭 (JI CHAOFAN) Chicken Fried Rice
鸡蛋炒饭 (JI DAN CHAOFAN) Egg Fried Rice
什锦炒饭 (SHIJIN CHAOFAN) Fried rice with shrimp, mushroom
     & chicken
蔬菜炒饭 (SHU CAI CHAOFAN) Vegetable Fried Rice
蘑菇炒饭 (MO GU CHAOFAN) Mushroom Fried Rice

SWEET TOOTH 饭后甜食 (FAN HOU TIAN SHI)
拔丝苹果 (BA SI PING GUO) Apple Fritters
拔丝香蕉 (BA SI XIANGJIAO) Banana Fritters
核桃酪 (HE TAO LAO) Sweet Almond Paste

MISC. SURVIVAL

请不要味精 (QING BU YAO WEI JING) Please, NO **MSG** !

菜单 (CAI DAN)   Menu

账单 (ZHANG DAN) Bill

我没有钱! (WO MEI YOU QIAN!) I don't
        have any money!

后门在哪里？(HOU MEN ZAI NALI?)
            Where's the back door?

等等 (DENG DENG) Etcetera, etcetera, etcetera.

Amoymagic.com

Hit the streets and experiment!

Chapter 13
Quanzhou Specialties

"The Chinese are of all peoples the most skilful in the arts and possessed of the greatest mastery of them. This characteristic of theirs is well known, and has frequently been described at length in the works of various writers. In regard to portraiture there is none, whether Greek or any other, who can match them in precision, for in this art they show a marvelous talent...

"...they had come to the palace while we were there and had been observing us and drawing our portraits without our noticing it. This is a custom of theirs, I mean making portraits of all who pass through their country. In fact they have brought this to such perfection that if a stranger commits any offence that obliges him to flee from China, they send his portrait far and wide. A search is then made for him and wheresoever the [person bearing a] resemblance to that portrait is found he is arrested."

Ibn Battuta, Arab Traveler

Quanzhou is famed for originating many unique Chinese crafts and traditions, such as fine silk, porcelain, stonemasonry, puppetry. And even today the streets are a nonstop variety show as wandering artisans make insects of grass, or intricate little figurines of colored flour, or in minutes whip our charcoal sketches or caricatures.

While you're in mystic Quanzhou, stock up on a few of these local treasures (and, as always, e-mail me with your own discoveries or additions). You can also browse online. Google led me to hundreds of fine Quanzhou company websites.

Dehua Porcelain—a limitless variety of fine China, as well as the ivory white porcelain figurines.

Dehua Famous Alcohol—brewed with herbs, it is "pure, mellow, fragrant, and "curative effect is prominent." Drink enough and you won't care if you're cured or not.

Hui'an Stone Stone Carvings and Shadow Carvings. Family portrait, perhaps! Take home a granite dining room set in your carry-on.

Puppet Heads. The hand carved camphor wood heads are rapidly giving way to mass produced plastic puppets, so buy them while you can (and while you can afford them).

Old Fan Zhi Magic Lees—a concoction of corn, beans, and over 50 Chinese herbs, it is said to cure everything from stomach and spleen ailments to indigestion, deng deng and perhaps dung dung.

Silk Flowers and Lanterns. Quanzhou Silk Lanterns are legendary. If possible, visit the city on Lantern Festival (15th day of the Chinese New Year). Check the internet for English websites of silk flower companies like Quanzhou Meifeng Gardening Co., Ltd.,
http://www.china-fair.com/2cpzl/fj/fjmeifeng/eindex.htm

"Silk is very plentiful among them...For that reason it is so common to be worn by even the very poorest there. Were it not for the merchants it would have no value at all, for a single piece of cotton cloth is sold in their country for the price of many pieces of silk."

Ibn Battuta, Arab Traveler

Qingyuan Tea Cake , made from herbs and tea, has for a century been reputed to be just what the doctor ordered for increasing appetite, strengthening the spleen, (Chinese seem to have a thing about spleens!), helping digestion, etc.

Anxi Oolong Tea—the tea that sparked the American Revolution—we threw it overboard during the Boston Tea Party. I can see why that would have tea'd the British off; I'd have been madder than the hatter myself.

Anxi Rattan and Bamboo—several factories produce quality baskets, shelving and furniture; you can even get it made to order. Check the internet for sites.   Anxi's Xin Long Handicraft company's fine English website has photos of hundreds of products:
http://www.fjneway.com/english/about_us.htm

Yongchun Preserved Vinegar, a black vinegar reputed to be one of China's "Four Famous Vinegars," has been a Quanzhou staple since the Song Dynasty. But I'd be careful with vinegar. "Drink vinegar" is a Chinese euphemism for "jealousy" and infers one's spouse is unfaithful.

Shishi Sweet Rice Cakes Dating from the Ming Dynasty, these are said to be some of the best rice cakes, but I wouldn't know. I prefer German chocolate cakes myself.

Hui'an Maidens Just kidding!

The Chinese Artisan

"I came upon a man in Amoy proper who with his ancestors had for generations made with rare perfection those tiny figures taken from Chinese legend and theater that one here and there sees fashioned in the streets. Made of rice-flour, each mass of dough colored a vivid green, red, blue, and so on with German dyes, the figures, about four inches long, are each spitted on a little stick, which when twirled between thumb and forefinger makes them kick up their legs and wave their arms like whirling dervishes...He worked with his son in the little mud hovel that had served his father and grandfather before him, producing forty figures a day when he worked steadily, setting them up in holes in a board to dry. As he was the only expert, there was a ready sale for all he could make; imitators made them, too, but theirs usually cracked even before they dried. He could have made more, one gathered, but being a true, even though unconscious, artist he insisted on always doing his best. The work was entirely free-hand; as the man put it, with his constant smile and an occasional gesture of his rough workman hands with a suggestion of the suppleness of the artist in the fingers, he just made what was in his heart. Real artists neither live in palaces nor wear silks in China. More than once I have seen one who outwardly was only a ragged coolie in a dirty street, sitting at a makeshift bench or table making these fantastic stage figures of colored dough on whirling sticks, or something else as intricate and full of life, while the crowd surged, children jostled and fingered, men quarreled noisily about him, and still his deft fingers plodded on, copying some artistic little thing directly from generations of memory and selling them at a copper or two each."

Franck (1925, p.198)

Chapter 14
Hotels & Travel Agencies

A small sampling of Quanzhou's many quality hotels…

4 Star

Quanzhou Hotel 泉州酒店
Great location, near historic Zhongshan Rd.; excellent cuisine.
Add. 22 Zhuangfu Lane, Downtown，泉州市区庄府巷22号
Phone: (595)218-2128   FAX: (595)218-2128

Jinjiang Aile Holiday Hotel, 晋江爱乐假日酒店
Add. Yangguang Industrial Town，晋江市青阳阳光工贸城
Phone: (595)566-6666   FAX: (595)566-6999

3 Star

Quanzhou Zaytun Hotel, 泉州刺桐饭店
My home away from home—beautiful garden ambience.
Add. North Tian'an Road, Downtown, 泉州市区田安路北段
Phone: (595)210-2222   FAX: (595)210-2108

Quanzhou Overseas Chinese Hotel, 泉州华侨大厦
Another favorite—perfect downtown location, EZ walk to
everything.
Add. Baiyuan Rd. Downtown, 泉州市区百源路
Phone: (595)228-2192   FAX: (595)228-4612

Quanzhou Huxin Hotel, 泉州湖心大酒店
Best chef in town!
Add. Huxin Street, Downtown, 泉州市区湖心街
Phone: (595)228-2888   FAX: (595)219-7889

Quanzhou Taihe Hotel, 泉州泰和大酒店
Add. Tian'an Road, Downtown (by stadium), 泉州市区田安路
Phone: (595)210-5888   FAX: (595)210-5888

Quanzhou Qunsheng Hotel, 泉州群盛大酒店
Very reasonable rates, spacious rooms
Add. Huxin Street, Downtown, 泉州市区湖心街
Phone: (595)216-6788   FAX: (595)216-6298

Hui'an Dapeng Hotel, 惠安大鹏酒店
Add. Dapeng Store, Downtown Hui'an City, 惠安城关大鹏商店
Phone: (595)737-7777   FAX (595)738-2471

Shishi Overseas Chinese Hotel, 石狮华侨大厦
Add. Jiu'er Road, Downtown Shishi, 石狮市九二路
Phone: (595)878-7108   FAX (595)878-1643

Nan'an Overseas Chinese Hotel, 南安华侨大酒店
Add.Ximei, Downtown Nan'an, 南安市溪美
Phone: (595)638-8888   FAX (595)638—9999

Nan'an Gold Deer Hotel, 南安金鹿大酒店
Add. Honglai Town, Nan'an, 南安市洪濑镇
Phone: (595)669-9999   FAX: (595)669—6333

Nan'an (Shuitou) Mingchao Hotel, 南安明超大酒店
Near Koxinga Memorial and Cai Minnan Village
Add. Xiasheng Rd., Shuitou, Nan'an, 南安水头厦盛路

2 Star

Anxi Overseas Chinese Hotel, 安溪华侨大酒店
Add. Lianyi Building #1, North Street, Anxi, 安溪北街 1 号联谊大厦
Phone: (595)326-6979   FAX: (595)326-6979

Yongchun Qiaolian Hotel, 永春桥联大厦
Add. 143 Huancheng Rd., Taocheng Township, Yongchun County
  永春县桃城镇环城路 143 号
Phone: (595)388-4202   FAX: (595)388-4205

Yongchun Hotel, 永春酒店
Add. 61 Huancheng Rd., Downtown Yongchun, 永春县\环城路 61 号
Phone: (595)388-6990 FAX: (595)388-2863

Dehua Cidu （Porcelain Capital) Hotel, 德化瓷都酒店
Add. Downtown Dehua, 德化县城关
Phone: (595)358-8188   FAX: (595)358-8988

Travel Agencies

International

Quanzhou China Travel Service, 泉州中国旅行社
General Manager: Li Zhangbin，李章彬
Add. #1 Baiyuan Rd., Quanzhou, 泉州市区百源路1号
Phone: (595)2282192   FAX: (595)218-2901

Quanzhou China Int'l Travel Service, 泉州中国国际旅行社
General Manager: Lin Zhenxing, 林振兴
Add. Mid-Wenling Rd., Quanzhou, 泉州市区温陵路中段
Phone: (595)228-5552 FAX: (595)228-1089

Shishi China [Int'l] Travel Service, 石狮中国旅行社
General Manger: Deng Baolian, 邓宝廉
Add. Jiu'er Road, Shishi, 泉州石狮市九二路
Phone: (595)878-7105   FAX: (595)878-1643

Domestic Travel Agencies

> **Suggestion!** You could easily miss out on a lot of the rich culture and history of each county, town or loality if you don't hire a **local** guide.   Contact the China Travel Service office nearest each location for a **local** guide.

Hui'an Tianma Int'l Travel Service, 惠安天马国际旅行社

General Manager: Wang Bingkui, 王丙奎
Awarded "Best 100 Domestic Travel Agencies"
Add. 1—3, Zhongzong Commercial Office Bldg.
Phone: (595)732-0008   FAX: (595)733-2889

Yongchun China Travel Service, 永春县中国旅行社

General Manager: Dai Dejun, 戴德俊
Add. #61 Huancheng Rd., Yongchun, 永春县环城路 61 号
Phone: (595)388-2863   FAX: (595)388-2863

Nan'an China Travel Service, 南安市中国旅行社

General Manager: Ye Yixin, 叶贻新
Add. #139 Xinhua Rd., Nan'an, 南安市新华路 139 号
Phone: (595)638-6213   FAX: (595)639-7138

Hui'an China Travel Service, 惠安县中国旅行社

General Manager: Rao Zheqiang, 饶哲强
Add. #1 Keshan Rd., Downtown Hui'an, 惠安县城关科山路 1 号
Phone: (595)738-7201   FAX: (595)739-8302

Jinjiang China Travel Service, 晋江旅行社

General Manager: Chen Jianmin, 陈建民

Add. #10 Qipai St., Qingyang, Jinjiang, 晋江市青阳镇旗牌街 10 号
Phone: (595)568-4176   FAX: (595)568-0840

Dehua China Travel Service, 德化中国旅行社

General Manager: Xu Wanyan, 徐婉燕

Add. #28 N. Longjin Rd., Dehua, 德化县龙津路北段 28 号

Phone: (595)352-2321   FAX: (595)352-2321

Dehua Cidu Travel Service, 德化瓷都旅行社

General Manager: Lin Hongfu, 林鸿福

Add. 1ˢᵗ Floor, Nanmen Cinema, Dehua, 德化县南门电影院一楼

Phone: (595)358-6896   FAX: 358-9552

Anxi Aviation Holiday Travel Service Co. Ltd,

安溪航空度假旅行社有限公司

General Manager: Xie Wenjiang, 谢文江

Add. #149 Datong Rd. Fengcheng, Anxi, 安溪风城大同路 149 号

Phone: (595)326-0999   FAX: (595)326-0989

Feedback

If you find a travel agency you'd like to recommend (or, warn others about!), e-mail me: **bbrown@public.xm.fj.cn**

And don't forget to check Sue's website for updates:
http://www.amoymagic.com

Miscellaneous

Traveler's Checks and Credit Cards

Traveler's checks can be cashed at any Bank of China, or one of its foreign exchange offices. Credit cards are accepted in many stores, hotels and restaurants. (A big change from the early '90s, when Bank of China took five weeks to clear a money order!).

Working Hours

Government and bank hours are, officially, 8:00 — 11:30 AM, and 14:30 — 17:30 PM (summer) or 14:00 — 17:00 PM (winter), Monday thru Friday. The noon interval includes the 3 hours lunch and xiuxi (siesta), when everything shuts down (except for post offices—which are open all day, 7 days a week!).

Our university gate guards, who zealously accost visitors morning and afternoon, leave the gates wide open and unattended during xiuxi (and when it rains). If anyone ever attacks China during xiuxi on a rainy day, we're doomed.

Amoymagic.com

Xiuxi--China's Siesta

Currency and Exchange - Changee Money!

Foreign currency can be exchanged for China's RMB (人民币, Renminbi, or People's Money) at any Quanzhou bank, and most hotels and guest houses open to foreigners.

Tourist Transport

Special Tourist Bus Lines

Quanzhou has two special tourist bus lines on which you can travel comfortably and safely to most of the major tourist spots. Narrators use Chinese, but perhaps for an extra fee you can arrange for an interpretor.

For information, call: 228-3842.

"One-Day Tour" Bus Lines.

Quanzhou has 15 special "One-Day Tour" bus lines, guides included, that cover major city tourist spots. The program is managed by Quanzhou General Automobile Transportation Company, Tourist Taxi Branch.

For information, call: 220-6220.

City Buses

Quanzhou's comprehensive bus network is convenient and cheap, and runs from 6:00 a.m. until 10:00 p.m.   The bus number, and places of departure and destination, are clearly marked above the windshield. The fare, either one or two Yuan, is paid after boarding.

Taxis

Minimum fare for Quanzhou taxis is 6 Yuan, and 1.4 to 1.6 Yuan for each additional kilometer. Pay the fee on the taximeter unless you are taking the taxi a long distance, in which case you can negotiate a set fee. In my experience, most taxi drivers are friendly and honest, but if you do have a bad encounter, report it at: 12315 (consumer complaints) or 258-8103 (taxi complaints). I've only filed one complaint, but got fast results! In the end I felt sorry for the guy (almost).

Emergency Phone Numbers

Fire or Police: 119

Public Security: 110

Traffic Accident Reporting: 122

First Aid Center: 120

Local Directory Assistance: 114

Consumer Complaints Hotline: 12315

Tourist Complaint Hotline: 227-4888
(Tourist Quality Supervisory Institute)

Tourist Inquiry: 160

Medical Facilities

Quanzhou #1 Hospital: 277-3906

2nd Affiliated Hospital of Fujian
Medical College: 277-0061 ext. 8041

Quanzhou People's Hospital: 228-5221

Quanzhou Traditional Chinese
Medicine Hospital: 220-7200

Quanzhou Children's Hospital: 219-5920

Special Supplement
Scott Ballantyne's Quanzhou Adventure

Scott on Chongwu wall (he's usually off the wall!)

Introduction

I am honored to end this book with an adventure written by one of Xiamen's most colorful characters, Scott Ballantyne. Granted, he's an Englishman, so he can't speak or write standard American English, but he gets his point across delightfully in spite of that impediment.

Scott Ballantyne came from UK to Xiamen in August 1995, bearing a degree in English Literature and an enthusiasm for adventure. For his first three years in Xiamen, he was a lecturer at Xiamen University and then, not being hindered by an American version of English, was recruited by the Swiss/Swedish conglomerate, ABB. Today, Scott is Sales Director for Global Sales and Marketing Manager.

All foreigners who have been here for a few years or more get asked the same question, "Why do you stay here?" and most of us give the same answer. Scott explained, "It is because every day I learn something new and interesting but as I learn I also help many people to understand the social and commercial differences between our cultures, and that is very, very rewarding.

Scott was instrumental in getting a whole village in north Fujian moved so that its children could go to school and so that its inhabitants and their descendants could live a better life. He rates this as the greatest achievement of his life. He has a book on learning English published in China and has written several novels and articles.

Having bought his own home in Xiamen, and married a local girl who didn't mind a fellow who wore a skirt (Scott's Scottish), he seems to have found his ideal place to settle.

Scott wrote an account of his Ningde experiences in my book *The Fujian Adventure*, and also a short piece for the last edition of *Amoy Magic*. I was delighted when he also agreed to write up his experiences in Quanzhou—never imaging it would take ten pages! As soon as I saw the length of his piece I got out the scissors—and then put them away. I present to you, unabridged (Quanzhou, forgive me!) Scott's impressions of Quanzhou! Thank you Scott.

Enjoy.

Scott Ballantyne's Quanzhou Adventure

If Bill is to be believed, Quanzhou is one of the best places in Fujian. As Bill is the most authoritative person on Fujian Province that I know, then he must be believed. However, when I visit Quanzhou, I find it hustle and bustle, noisy and dirty – and if that's what I want, I just need to go to my kitchen (I'm joking, wife, I'm joking). Actually, outside of Xiamen island, Quanzhou was the first place I ever visited in China – way back in 1995.

When I arrived in China in August, 1995, it was to take up a post in Xiamen University. There were a few others from USA and UK doing the same. After a couple of months, the Foreign Affairs Office of the University arranged a trip for the new foreign teachers (which they did a few times a year) and the first of such trips was to be to Quanzhou and Chongwu. Our leader for the trip was to be Alex, from the Foreign Affairs Office, and I think it was the first time that he had taken charge of a group of foreigners and I was convinced that he had been warned that if he lost, even one of us, or if any foreigner came to harm, he would be immediately whipped off to the Russian Front (which was especially bad as it didn't exist then). Poor Alex, he had no idea what he was in for, but fussing around like an old mother hen was not the way to treat a bunch of academics who had the spirit to find their own ways to China.

After he had counted us for the fifteenth time, he nervously ushered all ten of his charges (all of whom, by the way, were much older than him) onto the mini-bus (same as Bill's Toy Ota) and we set off around seven in the morning for the (then) arduous drive to Quanzhou. In 1995, the Xiamen-Fuzhou highway, which goes via Quanzhou, did not exist, so it was country roads for us.

Alex's enthusiasm for the trip exceeded all expectations as he excitedly pointed out things of interest to us on the way – things like, mountains (which were really hills), cows, goats, peasants planting rice and the odd jerry-built factories. Bottles of water were forced upon us at five-minute intervals, and a variety of dried foods ensured we would stay alive and he would avoid the Russian Front.

We arrived in Quanzhou very early in the afternoon and I remember thinking how big it seemed compared to Xiamen. The roads were wide and very busy, mostly with four-to-a-seat motorcycles (which I later learned were taxis). Every driver of anything with wheels was making a noise, hooting horns or ringing bells or just shouting. To say that it was vibrant would be an understatement and it had about it a great sense of industry, not in the factory way but in the way of busyness and commerce and bustle.

Our host in Quanzhou was the impressive Overseas Chinese University and we were taken straight there to unload ourselves, two-to-a-room in their guest hotel. The rooms were large and comfortable and I was quite happy, so far, with my first trip out of Xiamen.

After half-an-hour was permitted for us to unpack, we returned to the car park to be multi-counted by Alex and ushered into the mini-bus but not told where we were going, which is very much a Chinese characteristic – to take you somewhere but not to tell you where you going. It's a never ending Mystery Tour, and even requests of, 'Where are we going?' get responses of 'Never mind, you will like it.' I think they are trying to build up suspense and make it exciting for the unknowing visitor. Truth is, it usually ends up at a temple of some sort or another. Quanzhou was no exception, except that the temple was.

I had already been very, very impressed by the Nan Putuo temple on Xiamen island, but here was a worthy rival, Kaiyuan Temple. It was built around the same time as Nan Putuo during the Tang Dynasty but is quite different in its feel and surroundings. Where Nan Putuo has a slightly claustrophobic feel due to its surrounding mountains and huge rocks, Kaiyuan feels open and spacious. I particularly remember being fascinated by the two huge pagoda's which are about 800 years old. Actually, they are older, from 600 to 700 AD, but the stone versions we can see today were built in the 1200's.

The bright afternoon when we visited, gave a perfect light to the carvings on the pagodas and as I was walking around them, looking for the best photo angle, I spotted a young local boy, sitting cross-legged with arms folded in one of the lower-level alcoves, for all intent acting the part of a god. As I pointed my camera towards him, he jumped down and ran away, no doubt thinking that I would have some black-and white evidence of his naughtiness.

We spent too little time at the temple before Alex gathered us together and marched us, kindergarten-crocodile style, back to the bus, counted us again and took us to the next leg of our Mystery Tour.

The next stop was to a museum which may now be incorporated into the Maritime Museum, but at that time, was not. I am not sure if this is really the case and memory betrays me of the name of the museum, but I shall call it the 'Deadhead Museum' – just for want of a better description.

We were taken to a single storey building in which were housed a hundred or so grave headstones. Wishing to leave all puns to Bill, I will avoid the obvious. These pieces of stone were proudly exhibited in a form that totally confused me and as the accompanying texts were in Chinese only and our translator, Alex, used a moribund tone which he doubtless thought appropriate, I quickly lost interest but found myself musing on what inspires a person to even start a headstone museum. What kind of morbid quirk makes people do such things? I mean, there were headstones from all over the country and from different religions and with different kinds of carvings and languages on them, which I am sure is interesting, but how do you start to get fascinated by this? Perhaps my limited imagination is to blame.

After half an hour of translating headstones, Alex realized that his only audience had passed on centuries ago – every one else passing through the exit doors. He rushed outside, counted us a couple of times and headed us off to a bit of countryside.

There we found one of Quanzhou's most famous landmarks – Lao Zi – well, his statue, anyway. This huge stone figure of the founder of Taoism totally dominates the countryside. There is a mountain behind him but you do not see it beyond the imposing 5.5 meter carving. The other noticeable thing about the Lao Zi statue, and just as interesting for me in those early days in China, are the tour groups posing to have their photos taken. Every group, no matter how large or small, poses in front of anything remotely notable in China. These days, I watch with amusement and try to guess how many of the posers will do so with the two-fingered victory salute. There is always, always, at least one and usually many more.

Not too far from the statue, we were taken to the small Muslim sacred place of Lingshan, where we had a five-minute look at the tombs of the Muslim Saints before being crocodiled back to the bus and back to Kaiyuan temple and to the boat museum to see the restoration of a local Song Dynasty boat (or ship – I never know what is the dividing line between those titles – do you?). Today, the Maritime Museum is a must to visit, but in 1995, it was not what it is today and ten minutes was all that was required to see what it had to offer.

I know that Bill will be covering in detail, and far better than I ever could, all the historical places of interest in this area, and I, therefore, make no attempt to compete with his knowledge and skill. So forgive my brief and poor descriptions here.

Many years later, I was lucky enough to catch a Quanzhou puppet show. It was unbelievable and something I would never forget. What I didn't realize back then in 1995, was how much I was missing when Alex apologized to us because he had planned to take us to see the puppets, but on that day they were out of town, or closed or being woodwormed or something. Do not, when in Quanzhou, miss the puppets. That's all I will say on the subject.

As the Autumn light started to fade, we were taken back to the Overseas Chinese University Hotel, for Alex's favourite part of the day – dinner time. A few local university dignitaries had been invited to join us, so that we made up a comfortable group of two tables of ten. I found myself seated on the same table as Alex and I knew, from previous experience that Alex placed himself at the head of the food trough and that I was gong to have to compete to survive the trip.

Seafood, as you have probably learned by now, is an important part of diet in this part of China and Quanzhou is no exception. I cannot remember what we ate that night, but I do remember competing with Alex for the most delicious Xia – shrimp (or prawn – I never know what is the dividing line between those titles – do you?!). In China, where people can be very polite, Alex would be known as 'strong', in the west, where we can be not so polite, he would be called 'fat'. Like the archetypical fat guy, Alex liked his food. Now, when it comes to competing for Xia, the Chinese have a distinct advantage over us westerners.

You see, when I eat a prawn, or even a shrimp, I pull of its head, I fiddle around with its legs until I can get them off with as much as the shell as possible. Then, holding the fan tail, I scrape at the remnants of shell until it is ready to go into the mixture of soy and vinegar which I prefer as my little dish. After a little dunking in the soy vinegar, it goes into my mouth.

The Chinese, however, do it differently. They take the prawn, dip it into the soy or vinegar, put it into their mouths, jiggle their jaws around a bit and wonderfully spit out the shell. It mesmerizes me how they do it – I have tried many times and failed (I end up with shell on my lungs) – but it does mean that they can eat prawns faster than I can. Alex saw me as no competitor and he was right. So, at every opportunity, I turned the lazy sally (the moving circular glass on the table) so that the prawns were difficult for him to reach. That way, I got my fair share of prawns – in fact, more than my fair share.

During dinner, Alex hinted that he had a super surprise lined up for us after dinner, but like the Mystery Tour, he would not tell us what it was. Only when all food was demolished and all drinks drunk, did Alex announce that he was taking us to a disco.

Perhaps it is difficult for you to imagine how 'exciting' that was for us. In Xiamen, at that time, there were no pubs or bars (apart from the expensive bar in the Holiday Inn) and certainly no discos. In fact, I believed at that time that discos were unknown in China. Yet, here was Alex, promising to take us to one.

So, around nine o'clock, we were marched, single-file, by Alex, to another building. All the way there, Alex kept saying to me, 'Be careful, it's dark, be careful, it's dark, be careful, it's dark.' After a while of this, I replied, 'Alex, it may come as a surprise to you, but we have dark in England, too.' He shut up. Then, we arrived at a rooftop 'disco'. It turned out to be an open-air ballroom dancing evening to a few scratchy tunes recorded onto a tape. The foreigners were a big attraction and expected to whiz around the rooftop with a local beauty or two.

My prowess at waltz, tango, rumba or anything (except a smooch) that involves dancing with my arms around a woman, is not something I excel at – in fact, it terrifies me. I know that if ever I get forced into doing it, the local hospital should stand by with medications for light bruising, mild fractures or, if alcohol has been administered before dancing, then even serious leg breaks. So, I spent two hours watching others enjoy themselves while I refused ushering after ushering by everyone around me. I stubbornly planted my feet apart and refused them any rhythm or movement. Quanzhou residents may have concluded that Englishmen are killjoys had Prof. Charles Tyzak, a fellow Englishman, not spent the rest of the night wafting, light-footedly, around the rooftop dance floor.

Around 11pm, we braved the dark to be led, crocodile style, back to our hotel and to bed. I was sharing a room with Charles that night and we both got quickly off to sleep as we had an early start the next day for Chongwu – the old walled city.

Around three in the morning, my stomach prompted my bowels of some hyperactivity headed their way.

I found the bathroom, plonked myself on the toilet and could still be found there, groaning at six when we were due to get up. I informed Charles that I would not be leaving the toilet for the rest of my life and for him and the others to continue to Chongwu, and everywhere else without me. I was in agony.

'You know,' said Charles, knowingly, 'I thought you went a bit heavy on those prawns last night and that last one you had, the big one, certainly looked suspicious to me – I thought you were leaving it for Alex so I didn't say anything, then it was too late.' Thanks Charles.

He went down to breakfast promising to convince Alex to let me stay in the bathroom (or at least the bedroom) for the rest of the day. He failed.

'No way Alex is going to let you stay here alone. What if something were to happen to you?' he asked.

'The only thing worse than this pain would be death, and I don't mind that – I'm not afraid of it, I'm really not. Tell Alex that. Tell him anything, but let me stay here.' I pleaded.

He failed again and I was given a phial of charcoal pills, guaranteed by Alex to cure me in an hour – they failed – and I took the back seat of the bus, where I lay down and rolled around while the bus took me groaning to Chongwu.

The road to Chongwu is quite good today, but in 1995 it was known locally as 'Abortion Road.' Why? Well, any woman traveling on this road who was pregnant from anywhere between 9 hours and 9 months would have been rocked, rolled, jolted, shoved, shaken, bounced, roller-coasted and stirred until no baby could have stayed inside.

The road was several hours of sheer misery, even for those not as afflicted as I. When we thankfully arrived at Chongwu, everyone except me disembarked for a few hours (which included a lunch I felt inclined to miss) to view this ancient walled city by the beach. I saw none of it.

I slept for a while in the bus and prepared myself, at least psychologically, for the return torture. When everyone got back to the bus, they insisted on telling me what wonders I had missed and the sympathetic looks which accompanied their comments told me they were telling the truth.

The following year, I returned to Chongwu with a Chinese friend and was so glad I did. We walked on the city wall and were invited into the city to drink some tea, which we did. We strolled around the long, empty beaches and even had a swim. Today, Chongwu has recognized its value as a tourist resort and has changed much, but only on the outside. By that, I mean outside the walls. Some interesting gardens and statues have been put there (which I am sure Bill will describe in his book) and the area has generally been cleaned up and tidied up a lot. It is clean and inviting and interesting. Inside the walls, nothing has changed expect that the tourists cannot, I believe, get in, they must view its occupants from the wall.

However, on my last of many visits, a few months ago, I was allowed again into the city and then I went to the beautiful beach where I watched, fascinated, as the inhabitants took their boats and nets onto the sea, rowed into the huge waves in a half circle, securing the nets on the start of the journey and pulling in the other end on the return. Men, women and children all helped to haul in the nets and recover the catch before the men took the boats out again and again just as their forefathers had done every day for the past several hundred years.

I wonder how many generations will continue this harvest method of fish before tourism ranks more profitable and the old ways cease. It will surely happen, but I can say that I witnessed it the way it has always, so far, been. For that, I am eternally thankful.

The photograph at the beginning of this story shows me on the wall that surrounds the town. Whenever I look at the beach behind me in the photo, I think of Europe and how, with such a beach and such guaranteed sunshine, it would be so full of people sunbathing that very little sand could be seen.

Perhaps such will happen at places like Chongwu and Xiamen, but we are, at least, privileged to see it before it does happen. Enjoy every moment of it while you can.

Bibliography

Blofeld, John, *The Chinese Art of Tea*, Shambhala, Boston, 1997

Brand, H Shelley, *Memories of Old Foochow*, [January 23rd, 1932], in *Fukien Arts and Industries, Papers by Members of the Anti-Cobweb Society*, Christian Herald Industrial Mission Press, Foochow, 1933.

Brown, William N., *Amoy Magic*, Xiamen University Press, Xiamen, 2002

Brown, William N., *The Fujian Adventure*, Lujiang Publishing House, Xiamen, 2002

Cameron, Nigel, *Barbarians and Mandarins, Thirteen Centuries of Western Travellers in China*, Oxford University Press, New York, 1970.

Campbell, George F., *China Tea Clippers*, David McKay Company,Inc., NY, 1974.

Franck, Harry A., *Roving Through Southern China*, The Century Co.,NY, 1925.

Gibb, H.A.R., Translator & Editor, *Ibn Battuta, Travels in Asia and Africa,* 1325-1354, Routledge & Kegan Paul, Longdon, 1929.

Gleeson, Janet, *The Arcanum—the Extraordinary True Story*, Warner Books, Inc., NY, 1998.

Hutchinson, Paul, Ed., *A Guide to Important Mission Stations in Eastern China*, The Mission Book Company, Shanghai, 1920.

Ma Tong. 1983. *Zhongguo Yisilan Jiaopai yu Menhuan Zhidu Shilue* (A history of Muslim factions and the Menhuan system in

China).   1st edition, 1981.   Yinchuan: Ningxia People's Publishing Society.

Macgowan, Rev. John, *The Story of the Amoy Mission*, reprinted by Ch'eng Wen Publishing Company, Taipei, 1971. Originally by Butler & Tanner, The Selwood Printing Works, Frome, and London, August, 1889.

Mackenzie-Grieve, Averil, *A Race of Green Ginger*, Putnam, London, 1959.

Menzies, Gavin, *1421—The Year China Discovered America*, William Morrow, NY, 2003

Pitcher, Rev. Philip Wilson, *In and About Amoy*, Methodist Publishing House in China, Shanghai and Foochow, 1912.

Qiu, Huanxing, *A Cultural Tour Across China*, New World Press, Beijing, 1993.

Selbourne, David, Tr., *The City of Light—The Hidden Journal of the Man Who Entered China Four Years Before Marco-Polo*, (by Jacob D'Ancona), Citadel Press, March 2003).

Smith, Arthur H., *The Uplift of China*, London Missionary Society, 1908

Yule, Henry, Tr. & Ed., revised by Henri Cordier, *Cathay and the Way Thither, Being a collection of Medieval Notices of China* , Hakluyt Society, London, 1916.

图书在版编目(CIP)数据

魅力泉州＝Mystic Quanzhou/潘维廉著. —厦门:厦门大学
出版社,2003.9
ISBN 7-5615-2106-5

Ⅰ.魅… Ⅱ.潘… Ⅲ.泉州市-概况-英文 Ⅳ.K925.73

中国版本图书馆 CIP 数据核字(2003)第 077289 号

Quanzhou Magic
魅 力 泉 州

出版发行:厦门大学出版社
　　　　地址:厦门大学　邮编:361005
　　　　http://www.xmupress.com
　　　　E-mail:xmup @ public.xm.fj.cn
印　　刷:厦门新嘉莹彩色印刷有限公司

开　　本:889×1 194　1/32
印　　张:8.5
插　　页:6
字　　数:253 千字
版　　次:2003 年 9 月第 1 版
印　　次:2003 年 9 月第 1 次印刷

定　　价:20.00 元